Happy families are all alike;
every unhappy family is unhappy
in its own way.

—Leo Tolstoy, Anna Karenina

The Happy Family

Restoring the 11 Essential

Elements That Make

Families Work

Linda and Richard Eyre

ST. MARTIN'S PRESS ❧ NEW YORK

www.stmartins.com

Book design by Richard Oriolo

ISBN 0-312-26673-1

First Edition: June 2001

10 9 8 7 6 5 4 3 2 1

For our fathers,

H. Dean Eyre and F. LeRoy Jacobson.

They taught by example.

Contents

Preface

There was a time, and most of us grew up in it, when a generally supportive and nurturing home atmosphere was usually enough to make kids good kids and parents good parents. Moms and dads could take a fairly passive, leave-well-enough-alone approach to parenting. When problems did arise, solutions could be found, often from "experts" whose books took the tone of "If Johnny does this, you do this," or "If Susan develops this problem, try this solution." Parenting was largely a reactive process and a *defense*.

Those days are gone! The world has changed. Kids today hear a thousand voices we never heard and face a thousand challenges we never faced. Children have always been enormously impressionable, sucking into themselves the attitudes, values, and perspectives they are most exposed to. But the difference is that today they are exposed to everything—literally bombarded by the media, the Internet, and their actual and virtual peer group with all kinds of dangerous impressions and negative values.

This book, as its title and subtitle suggest, advances a whole new and much more proactive approach to parenting. Today's parents need a *strategy*, an offense rather than a defense—a plan for teaching values and for creating a home environment that includes the order, the commitment, the consistency, the roots, and the honest communication that the larger world lacks. These elements of family, which used to come rather naturally, now have to be fought for and carefully developed within a home by parents who understand the challenges their kids face and who have plans and purpose in their parenting.

The book has two parts. Part One is to help us understand *why* parenting is harder today and why we must take a more active approach. Part Two is to teach us *how* to take the proactive approach and make it work in today's world.

The purpose of Part One is not to present a full-blown sociological analysis of the times or a parent's manifesto on the needs and rights of families. Such would take both more scholarship and more pages than we have here. Rather, in Part One we look at what's wrong with our world from a parent's perspective and make a case for why we must be more involved. Part One is also a place where we parents (both the writers and the readers of this book) can express some of our feelings and frustrations about how difficult it is to raise children today . . . about how many forces try to pull our children away from the basic values and the state of safety that we want for them.

The mode of our time is *reactive*. We are exposed to and must respond to more outside stimuli than any other people of any other time. We react to media and to many agents acting upon us, and we react to our children's behavior rather than making conscious efforts to frame and develop it. After we have developed a clearer perspective of this new and reactive world we live in, in Part Two we lay out a proactive strategy whereby parents can reestablish within their homes the eleven essential elements of happy families, each of which takes more effort to achieve today than it did in previous generations.

The bottom line: This is not a book about how to change the world and make it a better place in which to raise children (although the closing section does include a sort of parent's wish list about what government and business could do for families). It is a book about how to change our parenting and our approach to our children and our families so as to counteract outside forces and maximize our own kids' chances to grow up happy.

—RICHARD AND LINDA EYRE
McLean, Virginia

ABC Parenting
Case Studies

‰

We call this first section an opening because it needs to be passed through before what's inside can be fully reached, fully grasped. In this section, we outline the organization and objectives of the book. Then we look at various types of families and at different approaches of parents . . . and suggest what Tolstoy may have meant when he said that "Happy families are all alike."

The Objectives of This Book

We see this book as a natural progression from our earlier writing. Many of our previous efforts have been how-to books on parenting (*Teaching Your Children Values, Three Steps to a Strong Family*, etc.). But it is harder and harder to practice better parenting techniques in a world that is increasingly hostile to families and in an environment that seems to work against the values most parents would like to impart to their children. Thus the attempt here to look at the why as well as the how.

The book has two objectives. The first is to help individual parents understand the whys and implement the hows. The second is to start a movement of sorts—to provide a common platform on which parents can unite and from which they can even perhaps reach out to change the institutions within our society that are working against families.

America's most basic institution, the family, is breaking down. And this breakdown is the direct cause of steep increases in other social problems: crime, violence, gangs, teen pregnancy, drugs, poverty, spousal abuse, child abuse, suicide, depression, homelessness, bankruptcies, latchkey kids, juvenile delinquency, school dropouts, and declining test scores.

If you doubt this thesis—if you're unconvinced that American families are breaking down as never before and that our burgeoning social problems are the direct result of this breakdown—we will seek to convince you of the truth of it. If you already believe the thesis (or once you do), we will try to explain why it is happening and expose the causes: hectically busy, overprogrammed lifestyles that leave no time for family; misdirected larger institutions that try to replace families; and commonly accepted false paradigms that confuse and undermine families. Raising children in this new millennium is a far more complex challenge than earlier generations of parents have faced. And we can't really follow the patterns or models set by our own parents.

For nearly a quarter century, the two of us have worked with and written for parents and families, and we are increasingly troubled by the difficulty of parenting and of successfully raising children in spite of the intense efforts being put forth by so many parents. We are both convinced that most of today's parents place as high a priority on their families as any parents ever have and that many are working at parenting with unprecedented effort. So why are marriages breaking up and families breaking down at a record pace and why are kids harder than ever to control and values harder than ever to teach?

We try to address these whys with some clarity and detail in Part One of this book because we believe that understanding the forces that work against families is the first step in saving families, whether we're acting individually as parents or working collectively as a society to stop the breakdown of families that threatens our whole way of life.

As you read Part Two—the solutions—don't get the idea that we think we've got all the answers. In the how-to sections, when we use little vignettes from our own family experience, we're just sharing what has worked for us. And raising nine exceptionally active and strong-willed children has given us a wealth of experience. We're trying to share with you some of what we wish we'd known earlier for ourselves.

We think it's best to read this book with someone. If you're married, read it with your spouse. If you're a single parent, read it with a friend, perhaps another single parent, or with a grandparent or someone else who loves your child. This way, as you read in Part One about the added dimensions and difficulties of today's parenting, you'll have someone to discuss these with, and you'll have someone to work and compare notes with as you implement the solutions in Part Two. Parenting is often a lonely and difficult business (as is trying to understand the world our kids are growing up in), and working at it and discussing it with someone else can do wonders for our attitudes and our motivation, not to mention our commitment.

Good parenting has never been more important than it is today because those who are now raising children, running companies, creating media, making laws, teaching, writing, voting, consuming—the adults of this world as it learns to start each new year with a 2—are this nation's last chance. If we continue to ignore (or take an aspirin for) the symptoms and if we fail to understand or combat the real causes, the America we have known will not exist for our children. But if we make families and values a priority, we can rescue our own happiness even as we turn aside the forces that would destroy our children's future.

A, B, and C Families

As we've observed, interacted with, and worked with parents throughout the world, we've developed an informal way of categorizing families—not judging them, but categorizing them. We call them A, B, C, D, and F families. The grades have to do with how much real happiness we see within families and with how much potential we see for long-range happiness. D and F families are severely dysfunctional: parents have essentially either left or given up. There is a lot to be said concerning D and F families, but this book is not the place to say it. For one thing, D and F parents don't buy or read parenting books. A, B, and C parents all love and care about their kids. What differentiates them one from the others is how they approach parenting, how they deal with the dilemmas and cope with the challenges of raising children.

Parents in families that seem the happiest don't necessarily love their kids any more or have any fewer problems, nor do they always seem to put in more time or effort. Rather, it is something in the way they *think* about their kids, about how long-term and unconditional their commitment is and about how much they enjoy the challenges of parenting.

During one month several years ago, we had some personal experiences that brought the A, B, and C categories into sharper focus. Early during that month, as I (Richard) was getting to know a client that my management-consulting company was servicing, I asked him to tell me about his company and his objectives for it. He laid out what I thought was a remarkably thorough set of goals and plans—starting with a series of specific long- and short-term goals and ending with some very detailed financial projections. It was all so good that I wondered why he needed any management consulting from me. I was so impressed that as we were finishing up our meeting I asked him a couple of personal questions. Did he, I wondered, have such clear and specific goals in his personal life, particularly for his family? "What are your goals as a parent?" I asked.

He looked completely confused. "My what?" he said.

"I just like the way you analyze and strategize," I said, "and I was curious as to whether you apply the same kind of thinking in your family as in your business."

"Well," he said, "I don't think you can. I mean, I guess if you're asking me what my goal is, I'd say it's to raise good kids, but how do you quantify something like that? I think we've got them in the best schools, and so far we've had very few problems with them."

The following week I had a completely contrasting experience. We were in Boston to attend my Harvard Business School class reunion, and one of my former classmates whom I hadn't seen for fifteen years came up and said that since I wrote parenting books, there was something he wanted to show me. In the right breast pocket of his suit jacket he had a copy of his company's mission statement—a carefully worded summary of the objectives and strategies of the medium-sized production company that he owned. From the left inside pocket of his jacket—"over my heart"—he pulled out an equally impressive family mission statement, along with the individual mission statements of each of his three children. "We've been working on these together for nearly a year," he said. "I get so much joy out of helping my kids figure out their lives. The world they live in is so fascinating. It's actually much more interesting than my business!"

Later that same month, we were speaking in a large auditorium full of parents at a hospital-sponsored community event. We tried to give parents ideas on and methods and techniques for everything from helping kids handle money wisely to setting up a more consistent system of parental discipline. On the plane flying home the next day, we got to thinking about how easy it is for parents to get excited about new ideas for managing and teaching children and for strengthening their families but how hard it seems to be for parents to stay motivated and really implement those ideas over the long term. Everyone is so busy, the effort takes so much time, and it's so easy for parents to just fall back to being the same kind of parents that their own parents were to them. Speaking to parents is a little like being preachers at a revival. Parents will come forward and get saved and all charged up about doing a better job, but often it seems as if they're looking for a quick fix and by the next week they will have forgotten it all or lost the motivation to keep putting in the effort.

So what is the basic difference between A, B, and C parents? Well, C parents love their kids, but they are just trying to raise them. There is no real strategy or goal or plan, and they tend to rely on other institutions—

the schools, the coaches, and other caregivers or teachers—to do the real work. They give their kids more things than time and tend to see their families as a bit of a burden because they are caught up with so many other pressures and priorities. When a problem comes up with a child, their first instinct is to look for someone else to fix it—a counselor or a therapist, perhaps, or a teacher. Their mode is essentially to put out fires, and they usually call on some kind of fireman to do it.

A parents, at the other extreme (the parents in the happiest families), seem to have a strategy and an offense. They have thought quite a bit about what they want to teach and to give their children, and they enjoy parenting—it is the center of their lives. A families seem to have certain common elements—commitment, communication, values, traditions, and a lasting and dependable kind of family infrastructure. Their children feel secure because they are surrounded by a certain consistency. They are aware that they are the first priority, yet they share in the family's responsibilities. A parents are genuinely interested in their children's world. They want to know about their kids' friends, their school experiences, their feelings; and these parents see it all as more of a pleasure than a task. They are aware of how different their children's world is from the one they grew up in. They have a sense of what their kids are up against, and of how many different voices and vices they are exposed to.

B parents are not as oblivious or escapist as Cs, but they are not as interested or as involved as the As. B parents want to prioritize their kids, but they view parenting more as a defense than an offense. They are reactive rather than proactive: "If I have this problem, what do I do about it?" And they tend to pretty much follow the same patterns and approaches that their own parents used with them, not really understanding the ways in which the world has changed. B parents read parenting books and magazines and are interested in techniques and methods to improve their kids' behavior, but they tend to look for the quick fix, a way to solve the problem so they can move on and not have to think about it anymore. Parenting is very important to them, but it is considered more a duty than a joy.

To use a medical analogy, C parents basically hope their kids won't get "sick," and if the kids do, they look for a "doctor" to perform an "operation." B parents find their own "Band-Aids" or "antibiotics," and A parents "vaccinate" their kids and practice "preventive medicine."

The A, B, or C designation doesn't derive from how many mistakes parents make or from how frequent or severe their children's problems may be. Rather, it is a measure of how much happiness resides in a family, of how many positive things parents are doing, consciously or subconsciously. A parents are far from perfect, and their kids are far from problem-free. But there is a certain consistency. The family clearly comes first. There are underlying goals and a positive purpose, and there are values and patterns that everyone can count on. There are, in other words, certain elements that always exist in some form in happy and functional families—specific things that allow the family to "work" regardless of the problems that exist in the broader environment.

A, B, and C Case Studies

To further explain and differentiate A. B, and C families, let's look at three case studies. Your own family may or may not have anything in common with these families economically, socially, geographically, or culturally. But you may find yourself identifying with various responses or approaches by the parents to their family's challenges. And you may begin to see more clearly what separates A from B from C.

As you read, try not to compare the specifics of your family to those of these families. Circumstances are not the point. For our purposes here, these families could be rich or poor, large or small; they could be headed by single parents; they could be blended or second families; they could live in the country or the inner city. We're not suggesting that these circumstances don't matter to families or affect them. But they do not dictate or determine whether they are A or B or C. What determines that (and the point of these case studies) is how the parents *perceive* and *approach* their families, their children, their challenges, and their role as parents.

The studies consist of glimpses into the three families' lives at different parenting moments.

The Calder Family

Craig and Cathy Calder have two children, Catelin and Clay, two years apart. Here are some of their moments during the past several years:

Craig has flown in late from another business trip and realizes while walking down the airport concourse that he doesn't have a gift for six-year-old Clay or eight-year-old Catelin. His job has kept him on the road and he hasn't seen his kids much lately; at least he can bring them something. Thank goodness Cathy's job doesn't require her to travel. She works long hours but usually gets home in time to tuck Clay and Catelin into bed. She took that last promotion even though she knew it would mean longer hours because it was more money and they needed the bigger house and newer cars. The extended day care is expensive, but they still came out a little ahead each month from where they were before the promotion.

Luckily the airport bookshop is still open. Perfect, Craig thinks. According to her last report card Catelin was struggling with reading, so the right book might help. He finds one on ballet—something he knows his daughter likes—and grabs a cartoon book for Clay and has both books gift-wrapped. He'll see the kids at breakfast in the morning and give them the gifts—maybe offering a reward of ten bucks if they can read the books before Craig gets home from his next trip on Thursday. . . .

. . . It's about a year later. Craig and Cathy have just missed another parent-teacher conference because their work schedules wouldn't permit either of them to get to the school on the prescribed day. It irritates Cathy that the school doesn't offer alternative times. One teacher does call to say how sorry she is that they couldn't attend and to report that Catelin has been caught cheating on a test. Cathy immediately calls both the school principal's office and the supervisor of the after-school program and leaves Voice Mails inquiring rather pointedly why they can't set up some sort of character education program that would include honesty and emphasize the problems and dangers of cheating. . . .

❧

. . . The following year Cathy is picking up Clay from the extended-care center one evening and is shocked to see that he has a black eye. He tells her that he fell down.

Cathy tells Craig about it late that night when he gets home. Clay has always been a timid kid, a natural target for teasing, but this is the first time they have suspected any physical abuse.

Craig says, "I should have done something about this long ago. I'm going to sign Clay up for youth football. We've got to toughen him up!" Cathy says she hates football and suggests the Cub Scouts instead. They decide that the two of them ought to talk it over with Clay, but it's tough because they don't have dinner together and Craig usually gets home after Clay is in bed. Cathy says she'll try to find a night next week when she can tuck Clay into bed and talk with him. Craig opens his DayTimer and finds a free Saturday morning late in the month and pencils in a trip to McDonald's. . . .

❧

. . . Several months later, Craig asks Cathy, who has come across town to meet him for lunch, whether she wants the good news or the bad news first. The good news is a promotion and a raise, but the bad news is that they'll have to move. Cathy's first reaction is "No way," because of her own job, but it's a big raise and Cathy finally agrees that perhaps she could stay behind with her job and the kids for a few months and look by correspondence for a position in the new city.

The only real problem, they remind themselves, is the kids. "Catelin has finally found a couple of really good friends," Cathy says, "and Clay's teacher seems to understand his hyperactivity and attention deficit disorder. Isn't there any way that they can give you a promotion that keeps you in this office?"

"That's just not how it works," Craig responds. "I guess there's more mystique if they bring in someone from another office. If I don't take it, I've labeled myself for the slow track and I'll never go anywhere. I don't think it will affect the kids that much if we move. There are other friends and teachers and good neighborhoods. The kids will get used to it. You probably won't join me until summer anyway, and they'll be starting a new year of school in the fall just like everyone else." . . .

. . . A year later, Cathy and the kids still haven't moved to join Craig, but Cathy has two good leads in the new city and it looks as though they'll be permanently back together by Christmas. Craig has been coming back for weekends a couple of times a month.

The phone rings. "Hello, Catherine Calder? You need to come down to the police department, Mrs. Calder. Your daughter, Catelin, has been caught shoplifting." In the days that follow, twelve-year-old Catelin tells a guidance counselor that she started taking things more than three years ago. "Sometimes I really want the stuff, but sometimes I just want to see if I can get it out of the store. It's exciting."

Cathy refuses to believe it. "She is just fabricating," she insists. "She's got an active imagination. She wants attention. Don't you think I'd know about it if she'd been shoplifting?"

That night she lets Catelin know in no uncertain terms that if there is another embarrassing call like that she'll be grounded for six months. . . .

. . . The following year Cathy and the kids have joined Craig. Cathy is straightening up thirteen-year-old Catelin's new room one day when she stumbles onto a letter to Catelin from a boy. She is shocked by its content. It talks about French kissing and the other "things I'd like to do to you."

Cathy puts the letter back exactly where it was so her daughter won't know she's seen it, and then she proceeds to worry about it for two days. She decides there isn't much she can do. She can't let Catelin know she's been snooping, and maybe it is just a product of an overactive adolescent imagination. Cathy makes a mental note to discuss it with a counselor at the next parent-teacher conference. . . .

✑

As you think about this case study of a C family, don't focus on the social or economic circumstances. The reason for the Calders' lack of concentration on their children could be affluence or poverty. The problems could be drugs or gangs instead of shoplifting or cheating. The Calders' passions could have been sports or the Internet rather than jobs or money. The point is, they have allowed themselves to become more occupied with other priorities than with their children and have essentially taken the subcontractor approach to parenting—jobbing out the responsibility for their kids to teachers, coaches, scoutmasters, day-care providers, and counselors.

There is nothing wrong with having help from all these sources, but Craig and Cathy are C parents because they're not really engaged or deeply involved in the priority of parenting. They love their children, they have every desire to raise them and to see them find happiness, but they are caught up in other things. They tend to go into denial about problems that arise. There is little structure or predictability in their family, little real communication or conscious teaching of values, and a lack of true commitment. Thus they are unlikely to have a happy and enduring family life.

The Ballesteros Family

Bill and Bonnie Ballesteros are the parents of Brian and Becky, just twenty months apart. They waited until their early thirties to have kids and approached parenting scientifically. They subscribed to two parenting magazines and bought a bunch of parenting books. Bonnie read *What to Expect When You're Expecting* before she was even pregnant. By the time Brian was born, they had dozens of methods and techniques in mind and felt as though they were prepared for virtually any problem that might arise.

Some moments from the last few years:

✑

. . . Bill and Bonnie are lying in bed worrying about three-year-old Becky and four-and-a-half-year-old Brian. "Toilet training and sibling rivalry," Bonnie says. "We've got two classic parenting problems, haven't we?" It seemed that the kids spent the whole day arguing with each other and competing for attention, and Becky was wetting her training pants constantly and then wetting everything else after she pulled them off. Toilet training had been so easy with Brian. "Well, maybe that's the saving grace," says Bill. "They're such common problems that there must be lots of books on them. I'll stop at the bookstore on my way home tomorrow." . . .

. . . It's a couple of years later. Brian is nearly seven and has been reading for a couple of years. Both Bill and Bonnie are worried about Becky, who still can hardly read a word even though they've gone through the same exercises with her. "We've got to change our rules about TV," Bill says. "Becky's got to spend more time with books—and let's tell her she can't start getting an allowance like Brian until she can at least read that first little book." . . .

. . . Fast forward four and a half years. Brian is eleven and Bonnie is glad that she's read how out-of-control tempers, bad language, and complete disregard for parental authority are parts of the normal behavior of early adolescents. She's read several articles lately that she can interpret that way. Perhaps her relationship with Brian isn't as bad as it seems. She can't remember the last time he spoke kindly or even civilly to her, but then she guesses she doesn't speak very nicely to him, either. At least they are open with their feelings, she tells herself.

Lately, though, Brian has started adding some pretty serious profanity to his disrespect, and Bonnie has decided something has to be done. She reminds her son of the time-out chair they used to have, when he had to go to his room and sit when he lost his temper or teased his little sister. "I think we better go back to time-outs, Brian," she announces. "Every time you swear at me, you're going to your room." . . .

. . . Becky is nearly eleven now and Bill is proud of her computer skills. "She's a prodigy," he likes to say. "She's better online than I am and I'm pretty good.

"It's how I relax," Bill says. "Surfing the Web just unwinds me after the pressures of the office." He spends at least an hour or two on the Internet nearly every night, pausing only to eat or sometimes to get the kids into bed. Becky likes the Internet almost as much as her dad and usually logs on right after school. When Bill asks her why she doesn't spend more time with friends, Becky says, "You can't see a lot of my friends—they're in chat rooms."

It worries Bill a little that Becky, a shy child who has always seemed a bit left out socially, can communicate so much better on a keyboard than in real life, and he is concerned with the violence of some of the computer games she plays. Still, Bill thinks, the best place for violence is in an imaginary game, and Becky is a lot better off (and learning more) chatting and interacting online than sitting in front of the TV. Bill has installed a filter that is supposed to keep the worst stuff at bay, and he's thinking of putting a two-hour-a-night limit on Becky's online connection. . . .

. . . Becky has blossomed as a fifteen-year-old and lost a lot of her shyness. Bonnie is driving her to her flute lesson when Becky suddenly blurts out that she can't see anything wrong with oral sex. Too shocked to respond, Bonnie just listens. "Nobody gets pregnant, you can't get AIDS, it's exciting, and it can show you really like someone. Everybody does it, even the president."

Bonnie's mind is racing. "Have you done it?" she wants to ask, but she's afraid of where that would lead. What would my mom do in this situation, she thinks. Then she remembers what her mom did do when there were questions about sex and decides it wasn't a bad idea. "Becky," she says, "it's not as harmless as you think. There are dangers in all kinds of sexual activity that you don't even know about. I'm going to get you a book tomorrow and I want you to read it thoroughly!" . . .

∽

. . . Brian is now an eighteen-year-old freshman at a liberal arts college six hundred miles away. Partly because of his tuition, Bill and Bonnie have maxed out a few too many credit cards and been forced to take out a rather large second-mortgage debt-consolidation loan on their house. At least their monthly payments are lower now. Still, it is very bad timing when Brian sends them a letter with a huge credit card bill enclosed. "I didn't ask for the card, Mom and Dad. The bank just sent it, preapproved, and I had no idea I'd spent anywhere near that much!"

Bill and Bonnie sit down with Becky, a high school junior, that very night and announce that it was about time the kids in this family learn how to take care of money. "We're increasing your allowance, Becky," Bill says, "and we're going to pay you twenty dollars for every A you get on your report card. You're going to have a bank account here for a couple of years where we can watch you. You've got to learn how to save and budget before you go away to school."

∽

As these glimpses illustrate, Bill and Bonnie Ballesteros love their children deeply and they are much more involved in their parenting than the Calders. They are taking the responsibility themselves, trying to find answers and trying to give parenting the time it demands.

The main problem is that most of their parenting is reactive rather than proactive. They read and think a lot about parenting, but mostly about how to solve problems. They are almost all defense and very little offense. As a result, they tend to emphasize the negative rather than the positive and to give attention accordingly. They approach parenting as though the job description were "catch kids doing something wrong and correct them." They also seem to be treating each child the same—trying to apply the same formula to each, although their kids are very different.

Bill and Bonnie also tend to look for a quick fix. They don't expect someone else to take care of their kids' problems, as the Calders do, but they want some neat little answer or solution and they often think they can find it in a book or from some "expert." Few would question their priorities or their commitment, but their rules and their forms of motivation—and even their communication with their kids—seem to shift and change and lack consistency.

The Alder Family

Al and Ann Alder have twins, Andy and Alyssa, along with Abraham, who is four years younger. Some moments from their parenting history:

. . . Al has been impressed with the way his product group at work establishes their yearly quotas and sets fiscal-year goals. He is a junior manager, just two years with the company, but he got to be part of the brainstorming group, and his supervisor spent an hour alone with him, asking for his ideas and inputs on what their group should try to accomplish during the coming year.

Al spends the next weekend talking with Ann and the kids about setting some family goals for what they want to accomplish in the year ahead. The seven-year-old twins get surprisingly involved. One of the goals they decide on is to set aside every Monday night for some kind of family activity. . . .

. . . The Alders have a tradition of going skiing with their extended family once each winter. This year Al Alder notices how pushy and aggressive eight-year-old Andy is around his cousins and other kids. He tends to boss them around and get physical with them if they don't do what he wants. And he is acting rougher than ever with his twin, Alyssa. Al gets concerned enough that he calls the third-grade teacher long-distance to ask how Andy has been behaving lately at school. The teacher says that Andy is a bit of a bully.

Al skis the bunny hill most of the next day with Andy and compliments him a lot on how fast he is learning and how brave and bold he is in trying new things on the slopes. He asks Andy if he knows what *aggressive* means, and they talk while they ride the lift about the word and about how good a quality it is in skiing, but how it could be a problem in interacting with other people. Al knows it is only a start, but he makes up his mind to stay on it and to keep the subject open with Andy until his behavior improves. . . .

⸎

. . . "Alyssa's such a sweet kid, Mom, but she's seriously underachieving. She could do so much better. I hate to say it, but I just think she's a tad lazy. I'm trying to think of better ways to motivate her." Ann Alder is talking to her mother about her daughter.

"Well," says Grandma, "strange as it seems now, that kind of describes you at that age." For the next hour, over pasta salad, Ann and her mom talk about Alyssa. The two of them get together nearly every month, usually on the first Monday, just to talk about Alyssa, Andy, and Abraham. Ann talks a lot with Al about the kids, but finds it enormously helpful to have someone a little more removed to brainstorm with. She and Grandma call it their five-facet review. They ask each other, "How is Alyssa doing physically, socially, emotionally, mentally, and spiritually?" They discuss each facet, and then do the same with each of the two other kids. Ann takes notes on any observation or idea that strikes her. By the end of the lunch, she has always distilled a couple of things to really focus on during the month ahead. She leaves feeling more clear about what she needs to do for her kids. . . .

⸎

. . . It's a year later and Andy seems to be having a harder time than Alyssa with the "Alder Family Rules and Responsibilities," a list of which is posted in the family room. Notwithstanding that list, Andy's room is always a mess, and the backyard, his household responsibility, doesn't get much attention. His main interest now is his basketball team, which practices three evenings a week and plays on Saturdays. Al and Ann sit down with him one Sunday and tell him how proud they are of how well he's doing in school and on his team. Then they review the reasons they have rules and responsibilities. They agree that Andy won't be able to go to practice until his room is reasonably straight. They decide to call the backyard Andy's zone, as in basketball, because Andy knows that you're not supposed to let anything bad happen in your zone.

ఎఌ

. . . Ever since Abraham could look at pictures and understand simple words, Ann has been reading aloud to him. She wishes she'd started earlier with the twins. The favorite stories of all three kids are the ones Ann occasionally tells them about their grandparents and great-grandparents—about when they were kids in the "olden days." When Abraham was old enough to talk, she began asking him after each story, "What did you like about that story?" and then "What didn't you like about it?"

When they watch a movie or a TV show together, or listen to a song, or read about a faraway place in a travel magazine, Ann always asks the same kinds of questions: "What did you like about it? What didn't you like? What would be good about living there? What would be bad? What did you like about the party? What didn't you like? What values did the main character in that show have? How are her values different from ours?"

She always asks the positive question first; part of the lesson is that there is almost always something good about most everything. Then she poses the negative question, because there is nearly always a negative side to every possibility. Ann wants her children to be good critics, to think for themselves, to have an opinion, yet at the same time to be tolerant and empathetic. . . .

ఎఌ

. . . Ann works with computers every day, so it is no trick for her to get into the memory of her home PC to check which Internet sites the twelve-year-old twins have visited. They have a Web filter that is supposed to prevent anything objectionable from getting through, but the kids are getting adept enough that they could hack their way through almost anything. She's talked with them about staying away from violence and pornography, but one Saturday morning as she browses, she discovers that they have found a fair dose of both. She cancels her plans for the day, then gets the twins into the car and takes them for a long drive. She starts the discussion by saying that she loves and trusts them and thinks they probably feel bad about some of the places they'd been on the Net, but that they are going to talk it out thoroughly. "We communicate about *everything* in this family, kids. I know this can be a positive talk. Everyone makes mistakes and I'm not going to punish you if we can talk it through. You better tell me everything, though, or we'll be in this car all day long!". . .

⁓

. . . Al has noticed that eight-year-old Abraham is acting even more disrespectful and rude than usual, especially to his mother. The only corresponding or related new factor Al can think of is Abraham's new friend Billy, whom he talks about all the time and whom he calls "really cool."

Al suggests that Abraham invite Billy to come with the two of them on Saturday to get a burger and look at basketball shoes. He wants to size Billy up and see if that might be where the attitude is coming from. . . .

⁓

. . . Ann is getting more and more worried about thirteen-year-old Alyssa. *She's the Ophelia syndrome personified,* Ann thinks, *trying so hard to look right, to be popular, to please everyone, especially her friends, and even more especially, boys.* Alyssa had been such an unaffected, spontaneous tomboy just a year ago, and now all she can think or talk about is clothes, makeup, image, and "who's cool." Her grades are starting to suffer and she's lost her passion for the piano.

Ann has been thinking about it for several weeks and finally realizes she already has an idea that might help. They have a family tradition of volunteering or helping with charity once a month but have let it slip a bit the past few months, partly because the kids have shown no interest. Now, Ann realizes, should be a time to redouble that effort. She signs up the whole family to help out at the Salvation Army soup kitchen, serving dinner to the homeless people staying at the shelter. Alyssa, after holding back and acting aloof for about an hour, really gets into it, asking questions and having some good conversations with the people to whom she serves the soup. On the way home she says, completely without her usual self-consciousness, "You know, there are some really interesting and bright people there. They've just had some bad luck.". . .

✍

. . . For years now, Al's been trying to have an individual "daddy date and interview" one-on-one with each of the kids once a month—on Sundays. On the first Sunday, it's Andy, Alyssa on the second Sunday, Abraham on the third, with the fourth Sunday reserved for any that were missed or canceled. In the afternoon they go and do something fun—usually what the child wants to do—and then they come home, sit across from each other at the desk in the den, and have "the interview." Al insists on eye contact. He always starts by telling the child that he loves him or her, is interested in him, and wants to know everything about him. Then he asks questions about school, about behavior, about whatever comes to mind.

Today, the first Sunday of the month, he sits with fourteen-year-old Andy and at one point looks him full in the eye and asks, "Son, have you or any of your friends experimented with any kind of drugs?" Andy glances down and mumbles no, but he's so easy to read. Al reaches over, lifts his chin up, reestablishes eye contact, and tells him again that he loves him, that he won't judge him or punish him, but that he needs to know everything so he can help. A tear comes to Andy's eye and he tells him about the party and the pill he tried. Al slides his chair around to Andy's side of the desk, puts his arm around him, and they talk for nearly an hour about the dangers of drugs, about which kids were in trouble, about how to say no the next time. . . .

✍

What sets the Alders apart is that they have developed goals and plans for their family. They have objectives and certain strategies, which they try to approach in a proactive way. Their mindset is one of an offense rather than a defense and of preventive medicine rather than Band-Aids. They look for the positive and take pleasure in "catching their kids doing something right." They praise and reward positive behavior.

The Alders are involved and engaged in their parenting and see it more as a pleasurable challenge than a burden. They have traditions and rules and are clear on the values and principles they are trying to teach. They insist on communication and make their commitment obvious to their children.

Perhaps most important, Al and Ann are *interested* in the world their kids live in, in the pressures they feel and the dilemmas and temptations they face. They don't assume their kids' childhood is anything like their own. They are aware of the forces that would poison their family, and they are, sometimes consciously and sometimes subconsciously, creating the antidotes they need.

"Happy Families Are All Alike"?

On the first page of *Anna Karenina,* Tolstoy makes a most provocative statement. He says, "Happy families are all alike; every unhappy family is unhappy in its own way."

When we first read that sentence, we disagreed with it on two levels. First of all, no family is completely happy or completely unhappy, so what was he talking about? Second, no two families, happy or unhappy, are alike anyway.

But maybe Tolstoy didn't mean it the way we first read it. Maybe he simply meant that there are an infinite number of ways to fail as a family, but there is only one way to succeed. Perhaps he was suggesting that there are certain essential elements that are a part of all happy families, certain things that buttress and protect a family from forces that otherwise would inevitably tear it apart, and that these elements don't change.

Indeed, all families that last and that produce security and happiness for their members do have some fundamental things in common, some elements that may exist in different forms but that are always present. Each element is a facet of love and a way of showing love.

From our observation of every conceivable type and kind of family, but particularly of A families, we have concluded that there are eleven such factors, eleven elements that always exist in some form in families that are essentially happy and likely to last. The elements are:

1. *Commitment* and recommitment (frequently stated as well as demonstrated).

2. A clarity of *purpose* . . . some kind of formal or informal (written or implied) family mission statement . . . a conscious parenting approach or strategy.

3. A true *prioritizing* of family and family relationships . . . personal time management reinvented to reflect family priority.

4. *Communication*—an insistence on it and a constant effort at it.

5. Family *rules,* laws, or standards.

6. Some sort of family *economy,* or a way of dividing family tasks and teaching responsibility and motivation.

7. Fun and lasting family *traditions* that involve humor and service.

8. Some sense of heritage, family history, and *roots.*

9. Efforts to help kids gain or accumulate an **understanding** of other people, of other cultures, and of the larger institutions that have an impact on their lives.

10. Correct *principles* being taught, including faith and belief.

11. A set of clear and recognized *values,* which are even more specific than principles.

In some happy families many of these elements are elaborately planned and consciously applied. In others, they are subconscious. But they are always there! In this sense, all happy families truly are the same.

In the preceding case studies, the Alder family exhibited these elements. The Ballesteros family possessed some, but not all, of them, and did not employ them consistently. The Calders might have agreed as to the desirability of each of the eleven elements, but probably have not taken the time to think about them, let alone apply them.

Interestingly (and disturbingly), every one of the eleven elements came more naturally and was easier to practice a generation ago than it is today. Commitment was easier because there were fewer other things competing for our attention. Families worked and played more together and had more shared purpose. True prioritizing was more natural because materialism and busyness were less rampant. Communication was easier because families and friends spent more time together. Families had clearer rules, better-shared responsibilities, and more lasting traditions because they were together more on weekends, at the dinner table, and other family-focused times. Correct principles were more ingrained in society at large, as were commonly recognized values. We put down deeper roots and we understood and empathized more with other people because we interacted more with people and less with computer screens.

Another reason the eleven elements were easier to practice a generation ago is that there were fewer forces working directly against them. The complex, fragmented, stress-causing every-direction-at-once lifestyles of today work against family commitment, prioritizing, and communication. The false paradigms and jaded world views of today work against correct principles, recognized values, and sensitivity and empathy toward others. And our large institutions (from big government and business to big media and markets) substitute for and undermine the basic unit of the family, thus working against effective family rules, responsibilities, and traditions.

This whole new level of difficulty for parents and families (and the hostility and growth of the forces working against families) was well stated by Sylvia Ann Hewett and Cornel West in their 1998 book, *The War Against Parents*:

> This [the erosion of the parental role] is happening not because parents are less devoted than they used to be. They do not love their children less. The truth is, the whole world is pitted against them. One of the best-kept secrets of the last thirty years is that big business, government, and the wider culture have waged a silent war against parents, undermining the work that they do. Some of the hostility has been inadvertent, and some of it has been deliberate. But whatever forces are responsible for the war against parents, one thing is for sure: parents have been left twisting in the wind by a society intent on other agendas.

The question, then, is how, in this materialistic, frantic, and often hostile world, can A families—those with the eleven common elements—exist at all? And how will they continue to exist in the even more difficult times ahead? The answer is that families will survive and thrive only by having a conscious strategy for the implementation and application of the eleven essential elements!

Most disturbing of all is the fact that B and C families are on the increase and A families are on the decline. The good news is that part of the B and C increase is from D and F family transition. More parents are taking parenting more seriously than ever before. They are more aware of the problems and dangers to kids; they are buying parenting books and going to seminars; they are trying harder. The bad news is that the other part of the increase in B and C families is from the decline of A. Fewer and fewer families are able to implement and maintain the eleven elements in a world where every one of them requires a more conscious and concerted effort than it used to.

We live in a world of the quick fix, and parents are looking for easy solutions, for magic methods and timely techniques that will rapidly solve their kids' problems and protect their families.

The root problem with so many B or C families is that they don't understand what they are up against. B and C parents too often simply haven't taken the time or made the effort to grasp the changes that have occurred in society over the past twenty or thirty years or to see what impact these changes have on families and children. Without an understanding of the forces at work against families, parents lack the motivation and the staying power to set up family systems and patterns that effectively combat the negative forces.

The reason for Part One of this book is to give parents that understanding, that backdrop of what they are up against. When a parent really understands this new world—sees how lifestyles have changed, how false paradigms have sprung up, and how larger institutions have knocked the family down to the point where it looks redundant—then he or she is motivated not to look for quick-fix ideas or methods, but to dig in and establish (and then maintain) a family that contains the eleven basic elements that allow it to withstand these outside forces and thus to endure, providing real and long-term happiness and security for its members.

Some parents will want to skip Part One, to get right to the answers and fixes and how-tos of Part Two. A lot of B and C parents, with perfectly good intent, will say something like "Look, I know the world is a difficult place, okay? And I'm scared enough about trying to raise a child in it. Just let's get to the eleven elements of happy families. I'm ready to evaluate myself against them and implement whatever's missing as best I can." The only thing wrong with this attitude is the very thing that separates Bs from As. Bs are not quite willing, for whatever reason, to be thorough in their parenting efforts and their family prioritizing. They want to cut to the chase, to find a shortcut, to jump over the questions to the answers and start implementing them. The proper sequence is first to understand, then to implement.

Having said that, having offered that caution and concern, we should admit that some parents need Part One less than others. If as you read through Part One you find that you're way ahead of us, that you really do grasp how different the world is now from a generation ago and feel you understand the forces working against your family and your kids, then skim and skip your way through Part One. Just read the parts you need to motivate you to tackle Part Two.

Looking Out, Looking In

Why is it harder to be an A family today . . . and to implement and practice the eleven elements? What in our society and in our world has changed so mightily and made parenting so much more difficult?

As you read, you may be sitting inside your home, much as we are sitting inside ours as we write. Let's look outside together, out through our windows at the world we now live in, at the world our kids are growing up in, at the world in which we must practice our parenting.

Think of our window on today's world as a three-paneled picture window, and let each reveal or represent one of the three massive anti-family factors that no other generation of parents has ever faced. Here's what we see as we look out:

Overloaded, complex, LIFESTYLES and false priorities that leave little time or energy for family life	All kinds of large, new INSTITUTIONS that undermine and substitute for the family	False paradigms and ANTIVALUES pumped into us by media, advertising, and societal "norms"

In the first panel, we see that the lifestyles of parents and kids are infinitely more busy and complex than those of any other generation. In most cases both parents work, and work longer hours; kids have more lessons and leagues; there is more entertainment and dramatically more technology. Other interests and demands turn our hearts away from our children, and there is little time or opportunity for quiet, uninterrupted family moments.

The second panel reveals how our lives are more and more controlled by large institutions that seem to have no regard for the small institution of the family. Big companies, big government, big school systems, big information, media, and recreation complexes are all so oriented to their own survival and growth that they take over the functions of families and compete with parents for the allegiance of kids.

The third panel emphasizes that we are flooded with merchandising and media, with information and the Internet; these are fraught with materialistic messages and make promiscuity and violence seem normal, if not acceptable.

The longer we stare out at today's world through our three-paneled window, the more we understand why parenting is more difficult now than it has ever been before. Each of the three factors impacts directly and negatively on the eleven elements that families need to be truly happy.

So here is the question: What do parents have to do inside their homes to counter or make up for what's going on outside of their homes? If we walk outside and look back in through our same three-paneled window, what do we see inside that can compensate for what's happening outside?

First of all, we'd better see a lot of focus and parental effort going on inside our homes, because there is a *lot* to overcome on the outside. And the efforts had better be directly aimed at countering what the world is doing to today's families and at reestablishing the eleven elements within our own homes. As we look in, our panels ought to look something like this:

Specific well-planned efforts to create a serene, family-oriented lifestyle that counters the world's chaotic "busyness," complexity, and false priorities	Specific, well-planned efforts to build a family institution and infrastructure that is a stronger influence on kids than larger "outside" institutions	Specific, well-planned efforts to teach strong values and correct principles, which overcome the antivalues and false paradigms of the world

The key words in all three window panels are *effort, specific,* and *well-planned.* Parenting is no longer something that can be done by instinct and reaction. It requires an offense and a strategy. But the good news is that this kind of positive, strategic parenting is both fulfilling and fun. Once parents understand what they are up against and have some clear ideas concerning what to do about it, raising children and creating strong families today can be the most fascinating and the most rewarding part of our lives.

Summary

Okay, what have we said so far? It's pretty simple, really, and all you need to do to keep it in mind is to remember the letters A, B, and C, and the numbers 3 and 11.

A families (proactive, purposeful, and effective) are on the decrease, while B families (more reactive and defensive) and C families (less involved and informed) are on the increase. Why? Because the eleven essential elements of families are being wiped out by the three new-millennium problems of totally overloaded parents' lifestyles, big new institutions that take over the roles of families, and false paradigms and antivalues that screw up both parents and kids. Part One is to help us understand the three problems and how they damage our families. Part Two is to help us beat all three problems by restoring and reestablishing the eleven essential elements in our own individual homes.

PART I

Looking Out at the Problems

Why raising children today is dramatically

different and more difficult—three powerful,

family-destroying factors that no other

generation of parents has faced

Family Decline and "Social Problems"

It is as though the world, particularly during the last part of the twentieth century, evolved in a way designed to threaten and weaken families. In fact, it sometimes seems like some force took a look at the eleven essential elements of happy families and came up with a plan to make every one of them more difficult to establish and maintain. That family-destructive three-part plan would have looked something like this:

1.   Suck people into such busy, materialistic, work-oriented, and competitive lifestyles that their priorities, commitments, and time for communi-

cation shift away from the family. This undermines the first four essential elements.

2. Make the family, with its traditions, rules, and motivations, redundant and unnecessary by replacing it with other, larger institutions that perform the family's functions and lure away people's loyalties. This eliminates the next three common elements.

3. Promote false paradigms and antivalues to replace time-honored religious values and basic moral principles and ethics—and to get people so selfishly wrapped up in themselves that they lose interest in the needs and perspectives of their families. This wipes out the final four essential elements.

If there ever was such a plan, it is working. Families are slipping badly, and as families go down, they pull society with them.

Too many kids today can rap but can't read. Too many know everything about drugs but can't pass chemistry. Too many have sex but have no love.

In America today, more teenage boys go to jail than join the Boy Scouts.

A generation ago a survey revealed that the seven biggest problems in one high school were: (1) talking out of turn; (2) chewing gum; (3) being disruptive, making noise; (4) cutting in line; (5) running in the halls; (6) dress-code violations; (7) littering. A survey taken recently at the same school provides a stark contrast. Today the seven biggest problems are: (1) alcohol abuse; (2) drug abuse; (3) robbery; (4) teen pregnancy; (5) assault; (6) rape; (7) suicide.

We call these crises social problems, but this is far too tame an appellation—too academic, too theoretical, too political. What we need is a word that suggests how dramatic and deep the dangers are. And maybe we already have the right word. Perhaps the word was presented in scriptural prophecy as the final verse of the Old Testament, where we are told that unless the hearts of parents are turned to their children (and vice versa), the whole earth will be cursed.

Burgeoning social problems are cursing America, and the breakdown of the family is precipitating the curse. The vacuum created by disappearing families sucks in everything from gangs to excess government. The public and private sectors—which should be supporting, supplementing, and protecting families—instead seem to be trying to substitute for them or to undermine them. Our newest, largest institutions—from giant corporations to information and entertainment systems—are creating misplaced loyalties and false paradigms that are destroying the oldest, smallest institution of family. And parents, hot in pursuit of professional and financial success, can find neither the time nor the inclination to put family first.

Social problems today threaten our future as much as economic problems threaten the former Soviet Union. So great are these curses, and so turned away are our hearts, that as we enter the new millennium there is serious doubt whether America as we know it will survive. Rebuilding, reprioritizing, and revaluing our families are the only alternatives to this country's demise.

Survive. Demise. These are extreme and desperate words—words we don't use much when talking about America. Especially since bomb shelters and the cold war have slipped away. But Tocqueville predicted our destruction from within. Illness rather than injury. Not threats moving in, but rot spreading out. Subtle rather than sudden.

The sickness we benignly and academically call social problems is so malignant that fathers rape daughters, so violent that children kill children, so epidemic that no one escapes. The shiny surface of America is pockmarked by poverty, riddled by racism, gouged by gangs and guns. The greatest, richest land paradoxically contains the most dangerous and terrifying places on the planet, places where life is cheaper and joy scarcer than in any third or fourth world.

And more subtle but just as sure, the sickness spreads through suburb and supposed stability, incredibly expensive, seemingly incurable, unfixable by courts or welfare—expanding, spreading. Preventable and curable only at the earliest stage in the smallest organization: the family.

Individual lives can teeter for quite a while on the edge, bereft of the ties of family and the anchor of faith and values. A whole society can do the same thing. "Re·valu·ing" has a triple meaning: (1) once again recognizing the transcending societal value of families; (2) personal reprioritizing of our families; (3) putting values back into our families.

But before parents can be fully effective in working on the micro, we must try to better understand the macro we work within. There are three categories of problems:

PROBLEM ONE: Overcommitted, materialistic lifestyles and wrong-turned hearts

PROBLEM TWO: Large new institutions that weaken and undermine the most basic institution

PROBLEM THREE: Proliferating false paradigms and antivalues

Overcommitted

Materialistic Lifestyles and

Wrong-Turned Hearts

Everything Relates to Family

We all entered life through family. And family will surround our exit. In between, family provides us with our greatest joys and deepest sorrows. Family has always been our main reference point and the basis for much of our terminology and metaphors.

- In theology, God is *father* and we are *children*.
- In history, the past is best understood and connected through extended *families*.

- In economics, markets and enterprise are driven by *family* needs, attitudes, and perceptions.

- In education, *parents* are the most influential teachers, and home environment is the most powerful factor in school success.

- In sociology and anthropology we conclude that society doesn't form families; *families* form society.

- In politics, all issues reduce down to how public policy affects private *family*.

- In public opinion polls, we reveal that *family* commitments exceed all other commitments. Seventy-five percent of us say our family defines who we really are (only 17 percent say our work defines us), and if we had an extra three hours in a day, 65 percent of us would spend it with family (only 7 percent would spend it at work).[1]

- In ethics or morality, *family* commitments teach the highest forms of selfless and empathic values. Lack of those commitments promotes selfish and antisocial behavior.

- In media, the things that touch us most deeply or offend us most dramatically generally involve *family*.

In nature, everything that grows is in a *family*, and people living closest to nature talk of mother earth and father sky.

Our similes, our semantics, our symbols—indeed, our whole frame of reference—is *family*. Yet as we move into the third millennium, the family is our most threatened institution.

Extravagant Lives

Despite the prominence of families in our heritage and mindset, there is less and less time and effort being spent on them. "We live extravagant lives" is how this is put in the Elton John/Tim Rice hit song from the pop musical *Aïda*. Indeed we do, especially if we define *extravagant* as complex, overcommitted, complex, fragmented, competitive, busy and rushed, and often excessively materialistic.

Most of us *think* that we have our priorities straight and that our hearts are in the right place. On public opinion surveys, nearly 90 percent of us say that commitments to family are "very important," and 82 percent say they admire someone who puts family ahead of work (while only 16 percent admire someone who will do whatever it takes for a promotion at work). On the open-ended question "What matters most?," 63 percent of Americans say family—far ahead of health or finances, which come in second and third with 19 percent and 18 percent[2], respectively. And by a 63 percent to 29 percent margin, Americans believe that life with children is richer than life without them.[3]

But compare the claims we make with how we actually live. Parents spend less time with children and more time with work than ever before. Divorce rates shock us, and an increasing number of people (including couples, married and otherwise) don't seem to want to have children at all, let alone devote significant time and effort to them.

Why is this? Could one credible explanation be as simple as the principle of dilution? When we try to do so much—to spread ourselves over so many activities, ambitions, interests, and demands—we dilute and divide ourselves, leaving lower concentrations of ourselves for each thing, including the most important thing, our families. How can it be otherwise when a parent is trying to keep track of 2 jobs, 500 TV channels, 30 favorite Internet sites, 4 favorite sports teams, 5 lessons or sports leagues, 11 friends with cell phones or e-mail addresses, 6 alternatives for next summer's vacation, and 3 mutual funds? It's not just the 2, 500, 30, 4, 5, 11, 6, or 3 that does it to us. It's the combination, the fact that the twenty-four hours in a day have not increased, while the number of things we try to stuff into them has—dramatically.

Sometimes it's hard for us even to imagine how much simpler life used to be . . . until we go somewhere where it still is. We serve on the board of a humanitarian group that sends "expeditions" to underdeveloped areas. When we're in a remote outpost in the jungles of Kenya, we're reminded of how basic, and in some ways how beautiful, life can be. Absent the attractions and distractions of the "modern world," families spend most of their time together and rely on one another and on other villagers and their extended family for their entertainment and amusement as well as for their livelihood. Days are long, time seems plentiful, and relationships matter more than

achievements. Even as you pity people for their lack of health care or bal-
anced nutrition or education or technology, you find yourself admiring them
for the relative simplicity and tranquillity of their lifestyles.

I [Linda] found myself sitting under a mango tree one day in the village
of Muambalasie, Kenya, watching a family in the dusty little yard outside
their mud-and-stick house. The father and two small daughters were laugh-
ing as they cooked lunch over a fire, while an older boy was helping his
mother crush grain into meal with a long stout stick. No one was in a hurry,
no one wore a watch, no TV or video games or cell phones were blaring or
ringing. I was aware, of course, of poverty, health limitations, and the lack
of options inherent in the dearth of basic technology. But as I sat there, I was
genuinely unsure of who has the best side of the trade-offs. They lack the
technology but have time to think and talk, a beautiful nature-oriented envi-
ronment, and a lifestyle almost completely oriented to family and friends.
We have the technology but lack the rest. (Read that last word with a dou-
ble meaning.)

What we didn't mention in the above reflection, of course, is that while
African villagers have no choice concerning their lifestyle, we twenty-first-
century Americans have multiple choices—more options than any other people of any other time. But family- and relationship-oriented lifestyle choices
involve far more than an answer on a public opinion survey. They involve a
reassessment of our situation and a recommitment in terms of how we will
spend our physical and mental energy, of how we will allocate our set, finite
amount of time across the frustrating and seemingly infinite number of
needs, demands, and wants constantly spread in front of us.

New Windows

We used the metaphor earlier of looking out through windows at the problems and family-negative elements of the world. Think about it now with a
new twist: Our parents, their parents, and their parents looked out at the
world through rectangular glass windows and saw their next-door neighbors. Like them, we look out at our world through rectangular glass win-

dows, but we turn ours on with a switch and they are hooked up to a Pentium computer or to the cable. In these windows we see everything from the latest Web site to a sitcom to an interactive game to another ad designed to make us think we need what we actually only want.

How much effect do our windows have on our lifestyles? How great an impact does what we see have on how we live? It has been said that there is no such thing as a truly independent mind. As much as we'd like to think that we are our own persons, that we take our own counsel, that we establish our own lifestyles and set our own priorities, independent of what we see and hear around us, it just doesn't work that way. We are all to some extent "programmable," and it is what enters us—through our senses, from those around us and more and more from electronic sources—that programs us. Advertising programs us to want more and different things from those we have. Movies and music and other media program us toward violence and irresponsible sex, and our whole materialistic, work-oriented culture programs us to compete economically and to set a high priority on money and power.

And if they program *us*, what do they do to our children? Children are incredibly impressionable. They suck in whatever values and behavior norms surround them. If we as parents do not make clear and concerted efforts to teach them values, they will absorb the values of their peer group and will set their priorities and learn their lifestyles from the media and the Internet. Forty-eight percent of American teens use a computer daily, and 21 percent admit that they have looked at something on the Internet that they wouldn't want their parents to know about.[4]

We can't just close our windows and isolate ourselves from the influences that counter our values or that carry to us the stress of materialistic competition. The electronic signals are in the air; they surround us and penetrate us hundreds of times a day with advertising impressions or impulses to do one more thing. The solution is not to block or stop what is entering our heads or our kids' heads, it is to start putting in what we want to be there—from values to the conscious kind of life we expressly choose for ourselves. Telling the mind what *not* to think doesn't work, anyway. If we say to you, "Don't think about an elephant," you find yourself thinking of one immediately. If we say to our children, "Don't go on the Net," or "Don't watch that program," they will do both at a friend's house. If, instead, we operate in the positive and say, to ourselves and to our children, "Think about these values and live a life motivated by family and relationships," then we control the direction we take.

In other words, we need an offense and a strategy.

Confused Means and Ends

What is the purpose of money? Ultimately, money has only one purpose—to buy things. It can buy necessities and luxury. It can buy comfort and education (or at least pay the tuition). It can buy vacations and second homes. Theoretically, it can buy time and freedom and security. But no matter what it can buy or what we choose to buy with it, money is a means to other ends. Money is useful only in light of what it will buy. Money is not an end in itself. Those who pursue money as such will lose the very ends that they subconsciously thought that money might give them.

At the risk of creating the impression that our heroes are all simple people from primitive societies, let us tell another personal story:

At one time in my [Richard's] life (fortunately a brief time), windsurfing was my passion. I even found myself thinking how great it would be if I could just retire and go live near some beach with my young family. Of course my time and my life were consumed with more serious things. I'd just become a full partner in a management consulting company, and my Harvard MBA mentality drove me to twelve-hour workdays; my windsurfing was confined to vacation time and an occasional weekend.

I had a client in Puerto Rico, and I found myself in San Juan one day, between meetings, walking along the beach. I watched a windsurfer for a while, riding and jumping the waves, and when he came in, we struck up a brief conversation, limited by his marginal English and even more by my nearly nonexistent Spanish. What I gleaned was that he was a Puerto Rican about my age, that he had a wife and three children, and that he and his brother were fishermen. They went out in the morning, netted what they could, and sold their fish to the market merchants each day by noon. He then windsurfed until his children got out of school. They played and ate together as a family. He and his wife helped his kids with their school les-

sons, tucked them into bed, and had the neighbor lady listen for them while they went out for the evening.

Let me see, I thought, he lives by a beach with his family, fishes in the morning, windsurfs in the afternoon, then plays with his kids, eats, helps them with their homework, and goes out with his wife and friends. It sounded familiar—a lifestyle a lot like the one I'd whimsically dreamed I could have someday if my company went public and I had a hundred million dollars.

Means and ends. We think money will buy us the very things that we are giving up in its pursuit. We pursue money as though it were the end, although we know it isn't. Our kids watch our example and learn from our model.

Usually, the trade-off is time for money. To get a little extra money, we give up time—family time, quiet time, meditation time, communication time, relationship time. And we do it especially during the early, intense years of our careers; these years are, just by coincidence, the very same years when our children are in our home and when, with more time and effort, our families could be flourishing. "Oh, but we're working hard now so we can have family time and family freedom later on," we say. It rarely works that way.

Sometimes we find ourselves longing to reverse the order of things: to retire while our children are young—to be with them while they need us and while we can enjoy watching them grow up—and then to work our twelve-hour days and make our mark on our career after they are grown and gone. But our obsession with work pushes us in exactly the opposite direction. Both parents are completely career-oriented to get ahead; the kids are farmed out to boarding schools or care providers in the meantime.

Money and material objects have become a way of keeping score, of competing, of proving our worth and our validity. And our work or career, the way we get our money, has become our identity. What is the first question we ask when we meet someone? "What do you do?" And we don't mean what do you do with your family or in the community or for recreation or for your soul. We mean what do you do for *work*.

This overemphasis on work skews our entire life. Again, the means and ends are confused. We don't see work as the means by which we support our family or the means whereby we provide ourselves with the time and resources for our relationships or our efforts at self-development or self-fulfillment. We see work as an end in itself, as our identity and as the thing that the other parts of our lives have to support. The family supports the career by moving to a new location where the job and the salary improve. Children support parents' careers by staying in day care or after-school programs so Mom and Dad can work longer hours.

Not only the bulk of our time and physical energy goes into our careers; the bulk of our mental energy goes there, too. Our best goal setting, our most creative planning, our hardest thinking gets devoted to time-consuming, keep-up-with-peers work, and we come home to family physically and mentally depleted.

How has twenty-first-century America become such a nation of career orientation and work identity? It doesn't derive from our European roots. In nineteenth-century and earlier Europe, work was perceived as a necessary evil—something you did because you had to and something you did just enough of to allow your real life and real identity of family and the pursuit of culture and self-actualization to flourish. The aristocracy, which people aspired to if they weren't part of, did not work at all, devoting themselves to higher pursuits like art, education, and travel. Americans clearly didn't come from that aristocracy. America was founded and built largely by working-class people who had to work for everything they got. Solid and desirable as this foundation is, it got seriously overloaded during the last quarter of the twentieth century. Our servant became our master. Work and career became the ends rather than the means. Lives changed in a hundred ways, virtually every one of them working against families.

There are no judgments being made here—and no guilt trips are intended. The materialism and obsession with work that so control our lives are not of our own making and are usually not of our own choice. Many family members are forced to work long hours and to hold down two or more jobs. Many would love to escape the treadmill that economic and social conditions have put them on. They did not create the cutthroat business environment or the social norms that make true satisfaction and economic security seem always just out of reach. The point here is not to blame ourselves. The point is to understand what is going on well enough to combat it or at least neutralize it in our own individual families. To do this, we don't have to drastically change our lives or drop out or quit our jobs or move to rural Alaska. We just need to set up a family program in our own homes that is designed to raise our awareness and our capacity in family-related areas—so that every day we meet the world on our terms, rather than on its terms.

Relationships, Achievements, and Communication

Trading time for money is not the only bad trade-off most Americans are making today. We're also trading relationships for achievements. Not relationships in terms of "boy meets girl and they shack up" (isn't it interesting what the word *relationship* has come to mean?), but family relationships—relationships between parent and child, between husband and wife, between grandparent and grandchild, between aunt and uncle and nephew and niece. Real relationships take time and concentration, the very things we are surrendering to work and career. Relationships also take planning—a focus on where they are going and where we want to take them. In a world where work is the passion and materialism is the paradigm, how much planning do family relationships get?

Part of the problem is communication. (Perhaps communication is always a part of every problem.) In families today—even good families with caring, committed parents—real communication is hard to come by. For one thing, communication takes time, which most families don't spend together. For another, kids' interests and orientations have never been more different than those of their parents. And for still another, many kids and many parents have become far more adept at communication with keyboards and monitors than with other people.

Some children today seem to live more in their cyber world than in the real world (in fact, they might wonder what is more real about one world than the other). A parent may have more chance of getting through to such a kid by sending him an e-mail, or better yet, by appearing to him in some kind of virtual reality interactive video game than by just sitting down and trying to talk to him.

And it's not only kids. The *way* our world communicates today can make us more adept at e-memos, faxes, cocktail party small talk, and sitcom language than at basic eye contact and voice-to-ear conversation.

The tragedy of that is that it can limit our power to address the problem of our lives. If we can't talk effectively or intimately with other family members, how will we create the kind of family program that can revalue and reconnect and recommit us within our families?

Worldviews

Some see the world geographically—continents and countries, latitude and locations. Others see it politically—groups and governments, ideas and ideologies. Still others see it economically—haves and have-nots, producers and consumers.

We see the world concentrically, centered on the most personal and radiating out to the most societal. The crux or core is the family, encircled by the concentric rings of the voluntary, private, and public sectors.

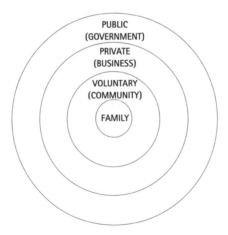

The family is the nucleus, like the center of an atom or the core of a tree, making everything else possible, providing the building blocks of procreation and nurturing from which all else is formed. The voluntary or community sector, the second ring, includes neighborhoods, churches, clubs, and all the other elective elements that encompass and link families. The private or business sector, the third ring, is the economy, the goods and services and enterprises that both sustain and employ us. The public fourth ring is government on all levels—all that our taxes pay for.

In an ideal society, the three outer rings protect, support, and supplement the core of families. More and more in our current world, they squeeze it, supplant it, and substitute for it, and turn parents' hearts and priorities away from the needs of their children.

Changes in the Norms of Families
(and Who Is Causing the Changes)

Changes happen gradually, and it's sometimes hard to realize how different families are today from what they were in the past and how different the world is in which they exist. Without trying to present a thorough sociological or historical analysis, here is an overview of these changes from a parent's perspective.

Prior to the twentieth century, most people lived in rural areas, on farms. Work/family conflicts didn't exist because farm families worked together, and family communication happened in connection with that time spent working together. The specialized roles of husband and wife, mother and father were accepted and recognized, so expectations were more clear and results more manageable. Children learned responsibility by necessity and learned to work by having to work. When chores didn't get done on a farm, the penalties or negative results were immediate and obvious. Delayed gratification was a way of life because no other way existed.

> I [Richard] remember reading my grandfather's journal. As a young father, he faced unbelievable hardships, working twelve hours a day as a farmer and carpenter, trying to make ends meet. Yet the more I read, the less sorry for him I felt. In fact, I began to envy his life. He worked with his wife and children. They had fun as they worked together—and they communicated and trusted one another. Their life had a simplicity and a quality almost impossible to find today.

During the first half of the twentieth century, as families urbanized and suburbanized, most households took on something of an adjusted and updated, urbanized version of the rural lifestyle. Parents still had fairly clear roles according to gender, kids were expected to do household chores instead of farm chores, and both divorce and living together before marriage were stigmatized. Families were still expected, both by themselves and by a broader society which supported them, to perform and provide the essential elements mentioned earlier.

All these norms began to change in the sixties, and the acceleration of these changes increased as the last decades of the century played out, finally reaching the stages of crisis and "curse" as the new millennium arrived.

The engines of change—the huge, seemingly irresistible forces that pulled the changes into effect—were the large new institutions in the outer rings of the public and private sectors. Their growth, their instinct for self-preservation, and their agenda for profit began to overwhelm the family.

To return to our diagram:

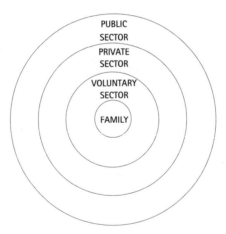

The public sector—comprising all our levels and branches of government and all their agencies, bureaus, and systems—has expanded and mutated so drastically during the twentieth century that its effect on and relationship to the family are completely different from what they were a hundred or even fifty years ago. Every element of the public sector, from our courts and our welfare systems to our public education and our tax structure, was originally conceived and set up to protect and serve our families. But as we start a new century, this outer ring looks less and less like a protective shield and more and more like a vise that makes it ever harder to raise, support, and have control over our own families. Government tax policy puts economic penalties on being married and having kids; legal precedent and court policy make it easier to run from family responsibility and commitment than to face and resolve it. Public schools often seem to undermine family values and parental authority. Welfare regulations reward families when the father leaves. And government as a whole seems determined to take over every traditional function of the family until parents essentially become redundant.

The business or private sector grew up to meet and serve the needs of families—from employment to the providing of the goods and services that households needed and wanted. But massive corporations, fueled by executive greed and stockholders' demands, have forgotten any loyalty or responsibility they once felt for families. They demand more time and loyalty from workers than ever before, and pay less for it. They want our loyalty and wish to provide our prime identity—often at the expense of our families.

Within the corporate world, certain sectors pose even more specific threats to families. Media entities undermine values and portray traditional families as outdated and irrelevant. Financial institutions encourage instant gratification and the overextension of credit. Merchandising companies use advertising to promote materialism and con us into measuring ourselves by what we own rather than by who we are within our families.

> Sometimes a half hour is long enough to make a parent realize what he's up against from the private sector. I [Linda] sat down to watch a sitcom with two of my children, but it was filled with sexual innuendo and profanity and it portrayed promiscuity and disrespect as appealing and the norm. During the program there were three car ads and two clothing ads, prompting one of the kids to say, "Mom, we really need a new car," and the other to say, "My clothes are so dumb. When can we go to the mall?" I got one phone call during the show (a welcome excuse to miss part of it) from our college student, who mentioned she'd received two preapproved credit cards that week in the mail at her dorm.

Even the nonprofit voluntary and community sector—traditionally an extension of family, or the village that it takes to raise a child—has become in many ways more an enemy than a friend. Our recreational and cultural complexes, from sports to the arts, have become so big and institutionalized that they divide families—some family members go here, some there, each with different loyalties and drains on his or her time. Evenings and weekends and other traditional family times are sucked away. Churches, community centers, and clubs, instead of being the family's strongest advocates and supporters, seem to be trying to substitute for the family. And a whole new institution of pop psychology and self-help puts such emphasis on *individual* fulfillment and personal freedom that it undermines family commitment and responsibility.

Essentially, all three of our "outer" sectors, which in previous eras (and in an ideal world) have acted almost as a uterus—protecting, supporting, nourishing, and supplying the family—have now, at the beginning of the new millennium, mutated into surrounding forces that imprison, choke, and suck the essential elements out of families, and that turn parents' hearts in the wrong directions.

How the "Outer Rings" Squeeze the Family and Take Away Many of the Parents' Roles

Back in the early 1980s I [Richard] went to China—it was a period when not too many Americans were getting in. I spent time in the countryside as well as the cities. What I observed was a country deliberately and consciously trying to make the large institutions of the state more important and more functional than the small institution of the family—to render the family redundant in the social scheme of things. While both parents worked in commune industry or agriculture, children lived in the commune care facility, where they were fed, educated, and collectively cared for. Some of the children still slept in their parents' apartment, but it was the larger commune that had the responsibility, the authority, the loyalty, the identity, the resources, and the vitality.

Today, in America and the rest of the Western world, responsibility and priority are also transferring from smaller institutions to larger ones, but here it's not by design or conscious intent. Most of our larger institutions are the creation of private enterprise rather than public control, and they were established to serve families rather than substitute for them, but the *results*—in terms of what is actually happening to families—are as dangerous and as chilling as what I observed in China. The family, and its basic purposes and functions, is being swallowed up, undermined, and rendered irrelevant by our larger institutions. The family is the victim, and the larger institutions, whether purposefully or innocently, are the culprits.

In our private sector, company identity and corporate loyalty have too often replaced family identity and loyalty. Our hearts and priorities are turned to our work. We're more likely to tell new acquaintances what we do or where we work before we tell them about our family. We'll relocate for a raise or a promotion without enough thought on how the move will affect our family. We're so worried about the positive possibilities of meeting a quota or the negative possibilities of not having the latest data processing system that we don't have the time or energy to worry as constructively as we should about our kids. Some companies, often motivated by their self-interests more than by altruism, hold out "solutions" like maternity and child-care leave, job sharing, flex time, work-at-home, and "mommy tracks," but these are usually aimed more at the goal of not letting families hurt the job rather than at not letting the job hurt families.

As parent loyalty and identity shift to career and company, other parts of the private sector are hard at work winning the loyalty of kids to various brands, or styles, or sports teams, or TV and music personalities and lifestyles. The media as a whole substitutes for families in the entertainment and social/cultural education of our children, and it cons parents into thinking they can make up for the time they don't give to their children by giving them more things.

The outer ring—the public sector—substitutes for and replaces families in even more obvious ways. Public schools take ever-increasing responsibility not only for the intellectual education of children but for their character and values education, for their social behavior, and for their after-school care. While it is, in many ways, admirable that teachers and schools accept more responsibility, it is a poor substitute for the full responsibility and involvement of parents.

The courts, the legal systems, the legislatures, and every conceivable kind of agency or bureau also increasingly substitute themselves into the traditional roles and functions of families. Courts are so preoccupied with individual rights that they ignore and undervalue family rights and responsibility. Children can sue their parents. Child protective services can take kids away from their parents on the hearsay of neighbors. Custody rulings seem designed to pull families apart. Legislatures keep trying to fix things with new laws. Government social services and welfare, filled with well-intentioned policies and well-meaning people, too often circumvent and disregard the basic purpose and position of families in their attempts to assist children. While there are family situations where the greatest need is to protect a child from a parent, there are far more families where the real need (and the real solution) is to help parents to take care of their parental responsibilities and stewardships.

> When we were named by President Reagan to direct the '80s White House Conference on Children, our first move was to try to change the name of the conference to the White House Conference on Children and Parents, so that the emphasis would shift from social agency solutions to parental and family solutions. The name change met with substantial resistance from many welfare social service entities who seemed to view parents as the main problem rather than the main answer.

Certain parts of the community and voluntary sector—sometimes the very churches and clubs and other neighborhood entities that should be closest and most nourishing to families—seem bent on making the family redundant. Plenty of activities and involvements are offered for kids, but precious few for whole families. Kids are encouraged to do things individually and with their peers far more than to do things with their parents and families.

Parents, particularly suburban parents in middle-class neighborhoods, seem to be following the "general contractor" model for parenting: As long as they get their kids to school, to scouts, to music and dance lessons, to sports and summer camps, to after-school programs, to etiquette classes and tutors and college test prep coaches, everything will be fine. These "subcontractors" will do all the work while parents just pay the bills (and work the hours necessary to pay those bills). Just get the kids to where they need to go and let the institutions of the public, private, and community sector raise them.

The biggest problem with this general contractor approach is that it doesn't work. What children need is the unconditional, even irrational love that only a parent can provide. They need the time and attention that is only fully meaningful when it comes from a parent.

The simple fact is that no other element or agency or institution can provide the unconditional, irrational love that children need to grow up emotionally healthy and happy. Other entities can give huge help and support in the raising of children, but none are adequate substitutes for parents and families.

I [Linda] think of our two oldest daughters, who each spent over a year in the early '90s doing humanitarian service and missionary work—and assisting in orphanages—in Romania and Bulgaria. From their letters and from the two visits we made while they were there, we realized that the basic physical care these orphans received was adequate. They were fed, kept warm and dry, and even played with occasionally by a nurse. Yet their dark hollow eyes and empty emotions spoke volumes about what they didn't get—personal, individual, unconditional love.

We were reminded of the studies done with baby monkeys who were offered a wire-mesh "mother" or a soft furry stuffed animal "mother" in place of the real thing. Even though they were given plenty of nourishment and a "fake" mother (all chose the soft furry one), none of the infant monkeys lived to maturity. They died from a lack of parental love.

The starting point in looking for real solutions is the acknowledgment that nothing can adequately substitute for real family.

Summary of Problem One

Over the past half century, our lifestyles have become dramatically different and more complex, evolving *away* from family commitment, family priority, and family communication. The public, private, and community sectors of society have evolved *away* from supporting parents with the family, and they now compete for our loyalty and our priority.

The Calder family (the "C" case study in the opening) was particularly victimized by this complexity. The parents were so busy and caught up with other things (and so oriented to materialistic priorities) that they had little or any time or mental energy left for their children.

Crowded, overly busy lifestyles undercut all eleven essential elements of families (see page 23), but they have a particularly devastating effect on the first four elements, as revealed by another look at the first pane of our window on today's world.

BUSY, OVERCOMMITTED LIFESTYLES AND WRONG-TURNED HEARTS, which get in the way of the first four essential elements:

1. Demonstrated family COMMITMENT.
2. Clear, family-oriented PURPOSE or mission.
3. Family as highest PRIORITY.
4. Time for good family COMMUNICATION.

The bottom line is that as we move into a new millennium, our lifestyles have become busy to the point of overflow with a hundred things that ultimately don't matter at the expense of the one thing that really does matter. And our hearts and priorities have been turned and pulled away from the "bull's-eye" of family by the "outer rings" of the larger institutions of society . . . which leads us into Problem Two.

Large New Institutions That Weaken and Undermine the Most Basic Institution

"Culprits": Whom Do We Blame?

Are families breaking up or deteriorating because we don't care about them anymore? A resounding no. Polls continue to tell us, as they always have, that we value our families above all else. Are families declining because we think them unnecessary? Again, a resounding no. Polls show that over 90 percent of us think they are the most important and needed thing in the world.

Well, if families are that strong, that valued, that important—if they truly are the most basic institution of society—what can break them up? Only one thing: bigger institutions. The huge private and public institutions that have grown up over the last half century, from media systems to merchandising giants and from public education to ever-expanding government, have had a profound effect on families, and much of it has been negative.

There are ten broad categories or types of larger institutions that must accept part of the blame. The first five, which sometimes overlap each other, are basically from the private sector; the next three are parts of the public ring; and the last two are within the community or voluntary sector.

1. Work and professional institutions
2. Financial institutions
3. Merchandising institutions
4. Entertainment and media institutions
5. Information and communication institutions
6. Political and governmental institutions
7. Educational institutions
8. Courts and legal institutions
9. Community recreation and social/cultural institutions
10. Religious, psychological, and self-help institutions

Obviously, none of these originated or were created to destroy families. In fact, all originally came about to serve families. But like a robot that grows able to serve itself and turns to threaten its master, many of the large organizations we have created now threaten the very small organization they were intended to serve. And the basic and ancient institution of family, instead of asserting itself and reminding itself of its primacy and priority, has let the massive new "adolescent" institutions crowd it out and con it into servitude.

While the family has been society's smallest, most basic, and most essential unit since the beginning of time, our present larger organizations are a much more recent phenomenon. Until the industrial age, the principal larger institutions were churches, tribes, kingdoms, countries, and other political entities that, outside of war, had little effect on basic family life. With the industrial age came urbanization and a whole host of larger organizations—financial, industrial, educational, social, informational, wholesale, and retail—which changed the very patterns of society and created a separation between people's work lives and family lives. In agrarian society, work was usually *with* family and was always perceived as *for* family. Now work competes with family, and we often have to choose between the needs and demands of larger entities and the needs and demands of family.

Besides that, our public and private institutions, while serving us well in so many ways, have gained frightening lives of their own and, motivated by self-preservation and growth, they have begun to squeeze and to supplant and substitute for the very thing that they were intended to strengthen, support, and supplement. They have taken over some of the functions that should belong only to families and fostered the impression that families are losing relevance—even that they are becoming redundant.

At the same time, sometimes wittingly and sometimes unwittingly, these larger institutions have created and fostered some false paradigms that have duped families into incorrect priorities and weakened their internal commitments. (The paradigm of work as our main identity, material possessions as our credibility, corporate or political allegiance as our first loyalty, and so forth.)

Mixed Blessings

In our family, what we try to do with our vacations is to get away from society as we know it. One summer when we had a particularly long vacation coming, we went for five weeks with all the children, high into the Blue Mountains of Eastern Oregon, and attempted to better understand our pioneer roots by building a log cabin. We were an hour's Jeep drive away from electricity and a world away from the kids' peer groups and from life as usual. We started in a tepee and moved into the one-room log cabin when the walls were partway up.

The whole experience was the perfect illustration of the friend/foe role-played by modern society and of the love/hate relationship most parents develop with technology and with the broader society. On the one hand, there were so many things we missed from "regular life." We missed the conve-

nience, the entertainment, the information, the communication, the readily available goods and services. But we loved the simplicity, the togetherness, and the unity we felt as a family. We worked together, we talked together without being interrupted by the phone, we ate together, we played simple board and card games together, we hiked and swam in a mountain lake together. We were one another's best friends and best helpers. Our family was the only institution there. It was both the hardest and the greatest five weeks of our lives.

In pointing a finger at "large institutions," in blaming them for the undermining and sometimes willful destruction of the smallest institution, we should be aware that we are making culprits out of our biggest beneficiaries.

So let's think first about what these larger institutions are—and about what we owe them. Let's consider what they have done *for* us as well as what they have done *to* us.

Our financial and industrial and business institutions have made a quantity and quality of goods and services available that could not have even been comprehended a century ago. Our business institutions have employed us. Our legal institutions have protected us. Our medical institutions have lengthened and improved the quality of our lives. Our media/ entertainment, informational, and educational institutions have opened the world to us and delivered enjoyment as well as enlightenment. Our governmental institutions have preserved our freedom and provided a safety net for people unable to care for themselves. All combined, the emergence in the twentieth century of stable, sustained larger institutions has dramatically increased our wealth, our access, our freedom, our awareness, and our health, and has enhanced our tolerance and our capacity to understand one another. They have changed the world, made daily living less harsh and less punishing, and given us convenience and opportunity that our grandparents could not have imagined.

So why call them culprits, these large and recent institutions? Simply because, despite all the good they may provide, they *are* endangering and undermining families. They do this by expanding and enriching themselves at the expense of families and by ignoring the values that are necessary to preserve families. They are thus the classic, macro example of a mixed blessing.

The question, then, is not how we can set the clock back or how we can eliminate these large institutions. Who would want to? The question is how can families successfully coexist with them. How can families take and benefit from what larger institutions offer them and yet not be swallowed up, or made redundant, or lose their sanctity or their priority in our minds?

Since these larger institutions did not even exist until the twentieth century, these are relatively new questions. How can we, as individuals and parents in the new millennium, revalue our families, accepting all the good that can come to us from larger institutions, while sidestepping the bullets of family irrelevance or abdication that they shoot in our direction? And how can these larger institutions themselves be persuaded to re-examine their policies and practices in light of their effects on families? How can they be reminded that they were created to serve families and that they themselves can survive only over the long term if families survive?

Big Taking Over for Small

Notwithstanding all the benefits they provide to us, many of our new, large institutions have become preoccupied with the preservation and nourishment of themselves rather than the preservation and nourishment of families. This kind of phenomenon is not hard to understand if we use some parallel examples and comparisons:

- A business situation where a large company, bent on its own growth, begins to view small companies as competitors and so seeks to eliminate them, or to swallow them up by acquisition and by taking over their functions

- A political situation in which the federal and state governments take over functions of local government and pass laws that supersede those of towns and cities

- A war situation in which a big country overwhelms a smaller one, using psychological warfare to weaken and then using its size to take over

- A medical situation in which an immune system is destroyed, allowing bacteria and viruses to take over an organism

The family is the little company, the basic local government, the tiny country, the organism. Big private and public institutions are the dominators, the destroyers, the hostile acquirers.

In many situations, those who have expended the time and effort to be in a position to run large public and private institutions have sacrificed a lot of family time and family focus to get where they are. Subconsciously, they seem to want us to join them. Subconsciously, they seem to want us as customers or as cohorts or as common sympathizers with their choice of lifestyle and priorities.

Speaking to a large audience of parents at a national convention, we walked them through the curse of social problems and the crisis of family breakup and asked them what they thought was to blame.

They all tended to blame themselves. "Not spending enough time with my kids." "Working too much." "Not knowing my children's friends well enough, or their caregivers, or what they watch on TV."

We probed further. "Do you really blame yourselves?" "How many of you think of your family as your highest priority?" Virtually everyone in the audience raised their hand. "Then why do you let these things happen?" we asked.

Then the tone changed. Hands went up all over the auditorium. "We don't let them happen!" "We don't choose how long we work . . . or what our kids see on the Internet . . . or the attitudes they pick up from their friends or their school." "We're the victims of it—it happens to us."

"Well, then," we said, rephrasing the earlier question, "whom do we blame? Who are the culprits?"

Now the audience began to release itself from parental guilt, realizing there were larger forces causing many of their family problems and hindering their efforts to be good parents to their children. The answers carried conviction and a little anger. "It's my employer." "It's greedy corporate America." "It's advertising and instant gratification." "It's all the easy credit and debt." "It's the schools—what they're teaching and what they're not teaching." "It's the movies and the rap music."

We made a long list of "culprits" on the overhead projector (it matched pretty closely the list of "larger institutions" earlier in this chapter), and we asked the next question: "What do we do about it?"

"Boycott them." "Write our congressman!" "Sue them!" But the answers were a little hollow. All of us were feeling our smallness and inadequacy as parents in fighting "culprits" so big and so powerful.

Then came the key answer from a young mother at the back of the hall. "It seems to me that we can blame a lot of these bigger forces, but I doubt we're going to change them—at least not right away. Maybe if we just see and understand what all these things in our society are doing to our families, we can talk to our kids about them and work out how to use more of the good and avoid more of the bad."

As parents, none of us is perfect, and it's easy to blame ourselves for every difficulty our children have, and to think that every difficulty we have in our families and in raising our children is our own fault. In actual fact, parenting is dramatically harder these days. For one thing, kids face more problems. Seventy percent of Americans think kids face more problems growing up today than their parents did. Only 5 percent think they face less.[5] Parents also face more pressures, and families are supported less and sabotaged more by the society around them. There are some identifiable culprits in this process, and identifying them is the first step in dealing with them!

1. Work and Professional Institutions

There is nothing families need more than employment and income. Yet ironically, more and more of the institutions that provide these things, in their own efforts at self-preservation and growth, have become a destructive force operating against the best interests of families.

Today, employers are more than a source of income and support. They are sources of identity and of image, and they exert more and more control over where people live and how people live.

C. S. Lewis said, "The home is the ultimate career. All other careers exist for one purpose and that is to support the ultimate career." Today, it seems the opposite is often the case. The family seems to be there to support the career, or at least to play second fiddle to it. As we suggested earlier, if the employment institution wants to transfer us to another location, we go, without very much serious thought about what the move will do to our family. If a promotion is available, we take it, without much consideration of how the new responsibility or new hours will affect family. (Even though most of us—61 percent[6]—think America was a better place when we had stronger attachments and didn't move as much.) When we meet new people, they're more likely to ask us "what we do" than about our families—even though 75 percent of us think it's our homes that "show who we are,"[7] and only 17 percent think it's our work.[8] Despite what we say we think and despite what our hearts tell us, we've become a society that lives to work rather than working to live.

In their obsession for self-preservation and profit, the work institutions of today are into downsizing, cutbacks, force reductions, and compensation restructuring, which have everything to do with the bottom line but nothing to do with responsibility to the families of employees. Second incomes and longer hours become "necessities" to families who are trying to live the American dream created by merchandising and financial institutions (which we'll get to next). The whirl of money and things and position and status and appearance and promotion and all the rest of it is what we read about, think about, talk about, and worry about, and in the process, the big institutions win and the little institution—the family—loses.

Let's be specific about how this happens: The damage is being done on four primary fronts:

- Wages, in real terms, are declining for blue-collar and nonmanagement workers.

- Insecurity is at an all-time high. Downsizing and layoffs loom as a constant threat.

- Workdays and workweeks are getting longer.

- Corporations are not doing nearly enough to assist and accommodate parents and to address work/life issues.

The growing chasm between the ever-increasing wealth and prosperity of U.S. corporate management (particularly top management) and the common employees and workers in those same corporations is shocking—and truly dangerous. The top executive in a typical mid-size to large U.S. corporation makes more than one hundred times as much as the lowest paid full-time worker in that same company. Top executives' pay goes up dramatically even as companies downsize. Examples abound: Levi Strauss & Company paid its president $125 million in 1996 and then announced plans in 1997 to lay off one-third of its U.S. work force.[9] Michael Eisner, the Disney CEO, was paid $204 million in 1996, a year when the median wage was $33,500—meaning a regular person would have to work 6,182 years to earn what Eisner earned in one year.[10] At IBM in 1995, right after 60,000 workers were fired, the company gave $5.8 million in bonuses to its top five executives. The IBM chairman received a $2.6 million bonus on top of his normal compensation of $12.4 million, yet that same year his secretaries were told to expect salary cuts of 36 percent.[11]

Real wages (adjusted for inflation) for production and nonsupervisory workers (80 percent of all workers and the vast majority of parents) declined 10 percent between the mid-seventies and the mid-nineties.[12] The median worker's salary (the middle of the middle class) fell 5 percent between 1989 and 1997.[13] That trend, and the constant increases in pay and perks to top management, continues as we start a new millennium. Never before in American history have the majority of American workers suffered real-wage reductions while the per capita gross domestic product was advancing.[14] By contrast, in the thirty years between the mid-forties and the mid-seventies, every sector of society—rich, middle-class, and poor—experienced at least a doubling of real income, and the bottom fifth advanced faster than the top fifth.

With all the talk we hear about a kinder corporate America offering flexible work schedules and other stress-busting programs, most companies still go by the old rules. USA Today, in 1999, said, "Mounting evidence shows companies are not adopting changes widely touted as key to helping workers balancing work and family. Family-friendly programs such as job-sharing, shorter workweeks, elder-care help, and on-site child care are hardly the rage"[15] And a survey of corporate human resource officials shows that 64 percent think their companies don't make a real effort to inform employees of their family-friendly programs that *are* available.

Managers' minds are on profit margins, competitive edge, mergers and acquisitions, and the bottom line, not on the human, personal, and family needs of their employees.

With the ever-present culture of down-sizing and layoffs, employees are understandably hesitant to ask either for better wages or for more family-friendly benefits. In the mid-nineties, a nationwide poll indicated that 40 percent of American workers worried that they might be fully or partially laid off or have their wages reduced. During the two previous years, one-quarter of the poll respondents actually *had* either been laid off or reduced or had taken a pay cut. There were over 600,000 announced firings in 1995 (a year of economic recovery and progress), involving some of America's most prestigious corporations. (AT&T fired 40,000 people that year, GM 75,000, IBM 60,000, Sears Roebuck 50,000.[16])

A significant minority of downsized workers fail to find new jobs, and many of those who do end up with a lower-paying job. In fact, a labor department study showed that only 71 percent of downsized workers find another job within two years, and less than half of those find a job that pays as well as the one they lost.[17]

Even as American workers get lower wages and less job security, they are working longer hours and working more on weekends. The number of adult Americans who hold two or more jobs went up 64.6 percent between the early fifties and the late nineties.[18] Compared with twenty years ago, the average American is now on the job an additional 163 hours a year—essentially working a full month longer![19] Imagine the family devastation that results from this extra work time—in a society where both parents usually work. As in so many things, the children are the real losers.

In the previous century, the societal goal seemed to be the shortening and limiting of the workweek. Unions played a huge role in achieving this goal and the goal of more just wages. Today most unions are all but emasculated. By the nineties, there were more than 1,500 corporation consultants earning $500 million per year to help corporations bust unions—advertising their services with words like "we will show you how to screw your employees . . . how to keep them smiling on low pay, how to maneuver them into low-paying jobs they are afraid to walk away from."[20]

These troublesome trends in wages, job security, hours, and other work/life issues are evident throughout the private sector. And within several subcategories of business—particularly the financial, merchandising, media, and information institutions—additional factors are at work to undermine and threaten families.

2. Financial Institutions

Ever since there has been money, there have been bankers or their equivalent—people who borrow and lend money. But it is only recently that financial institutions have become so huge and so influential that they exert major control over many aspects of our personal and our societal lives. They have, in essence, created a credit society and a debt culture in which families spend before they earn and in which we are oriented to instant gratification at almost every level.

> *Credit cards, pre-approved, arrive in the mail—even to college freshmen and eighteen-year-olds who have no clue how to use credit. One of the things we sent with our oldest daughter when she left for her freshman year at Wellesley College outside Boston was a good pair of scissors and an admonition to cut in half every credit card she received in the mail. She told us later that she had used those scissors more than a dozen times. Her roommate had never borrowed the scissors and presented her parents with a $5,000 bill when she went home for Christmas.*

People buy everything from cars to Christmas presents based on the amount of the monthly payment rather than on the total price. Often they do not even know the full ticket cost, let alone the total amount they will ultimately pay, including interest.

Parents, in an effort to "keep up with the Joneses" and to give their children all they need, become debt-ridden and, in the process, teach dangerous financial principles to their kids even as they spend less and less time with their families and work longer and longer hours to pay their bills.

It has been observed that you can tell a lot about a society by which of its sectors is building the biggest or most magnificent edifices. For centuries, churches and cathedrals and synagogues and temples were the most impressive structures. Then there was a span of years when government buildings seemed to be the biggest and most opulent. Then the skyscrapers, plants, and corporate headquarters of major industrial corporations. Today, many would argue that the most opulent and pretentious new buildings are banks and other financial institutions. The competition between them and their push for growth and stockholder profit has been their incentive to create a debt-and-credit mentality that is hugely destructive to families.

3. Merchandising Institutions

Of course there have always been salesmen and sales-oriented organizations, and the very essence of commerce and economy at any level is the promotion and marketing of goods and services. Certainly a desire for things—a materialism in some form or other—has existed since the beginning of time.

But again, what has changed everything is the emergence of huge and influential marketing and advertising institutions whose single goal or reason for existence is to sell more product without regard to the true needs or buying capacities of the consumer.

> *A close friend of ours, chairman of a worldwide ad agency, is uncommonly objective and frank about his profession. "The basic goal of advertising," he says, "is to make people think they need what they really only want." Think about the implications of that. Hundreds of advertising impressions, from billboards to radio and TV spots, come at us every day, each carefully designed to make us dissatisfied with what we have, how we look, where we are, what we do, how we live.*

Because of the messages of advertising, people tend to measure themselves (and others) more by what they have than by what they are. Appearances supersede substance. Things become more important than people.

Acquisition and achievements are given more time and more effort than relationships and family.

Occasionally an ad plays on warm family images, but most often glitz, social status, materialism, and "freedom" from burden or obligation constitute the portrayed ideal. Our own workaday family responsibilities look boring and mundane next to these advertising images.

So parents and families take a double hit: (1) They are prompted to be dissatisfied with simple, family-oriented lifestyles, and (2) they are enticed to spend more on things that compete with family needs.

And it's not just advertising. The huge American merchandising machine includes everything from infomercials, home shopping channels, and online purchasing to wholesale clubs, rebates, and high-powered retail promotions. On the one hand, all these service our consumer needs and can make life more convenient; but on the other hand, they fill our lives with complexity, with unmet "needs," and with debt—robbing us of family time and family awareness and priority in the process.

In marketing parlance, there is a distinction made between "demand pull" and "product push." Sometimes a real need or demand "pulls" or creates a product and a distribution system. Other times a product "pushes" or creates its own interest and market. Before the twentieth century, most of our economy operated primarily by demand pull. But with the emergence of today's huge merchandising/advertising institutions, there is a massive shift to product push, and the "products" range from unlimited things to styles to programming to attitudes. And very few of them enhance the family—in fact, most compete with and de-prioritize family and neighborhood relationships.

Merchandising institutions, from agencies to the marketing arms of retail and industrial giants, measure themselves on how much product they can sell and how much money they can extract from people—from families. And it's not just money they extract, it's time, and attention, and priorities, much of which might otherwise go to children and to the maintenance and strengthening of family relationships.

Naturally this "merchandising culprit" is linked to the "financial culprit." The wants that are cultivated and encouraged by the merchandisers lead to the need for the easy credit that is extended by the financials. The one-two punch works particularly well on families. Children are often the prime target of advertisers, and parents overextend their credit to give their children things to make up for the very time and attention they are putting elsewhere.

4. Entertainment and Media Institutions

Entertainment has existed as long as people have, and the messages of song and dance, of theater, of the visual arts, and even of sports have always been varied and diverse—some of them derogatory or dangerous to the family. Various ways of reporting on events or "news" have also existed forever. But it is only recently that entertainment and news have combined with electronic media technology and become an institution so vast, so powerful, and so centralized that its messages could threaten and undermine families and the values that sustain families on a wide, even global scale.

On the positive side, entertainment media, from movies to TV to music, brings families together, gives them a shared experience, helps them communicate, and can at times uplift and even inspire them. And news media keeps us informed and up-to-date like never before. Yet at the same time, our media today is so pervasive and so addictive that it takes time away from families and substitutes for communication within families, even as it douses us with content that desensitizes us to violence, to casual sex, and to other destroyers of family.

When soap operas (or sit-coms) portray promiscuous teenage sex as the norm, it becomes the norm. When movies or TV dramas portray indiscriminate violence as commonplace, it becomes commonplace. When rap songs portray hatred and bizarre acts as the thing to feel and the things to do, they become exactly that for millions. When news covers only the sensational or the violent, we think that's how the world is. And when irresponsible or valueless behavior is presented without any reference or connection to consequences, young people (and older ones, too, for that matter) begin to believe those behaviors are normal and acceptable.

In a television debate on who should take responsibility for a horrendous high school murder and suicide tragedy, a producer/director type was insisting that it was unfair to blame the media. Where, then, asked his opponent, did the shooters get their graphic images of dark gun violence, spurting blood, and exploding bodies? Did they get those images from their parents? From their school? From their church?

We know how susceptible the human mind is, especially the young mind, to visual and audio suggestion. It's why companies are willing to pay a million dollars for a thirty-second impression during the Super Bowl. Yet we continue to allow violent, antisocial images to flow at our children several times a day.

Teen pregnancy and sexually transmitted diseases are at epidemic proportions as our kids watch nightly sit-coms where people jump into bed on the first date and sex is generally treated as a form of recreation. Routine divorce, single parenting, and various alternative lifestyles get far more play than stable marriages and families—so much so that someone really committed to his marriage and family might tune in for an evening of standard-fare TV and conclude that he was a dinosaur, hopelessly old-fashioned and out of touch.

Daytime TV talk shows, in their quest for ratings, compete against one another in terms of which can find and present the most irresponsible and bizarre behavior. In the process they lower the bar of what is acceptable and undermine the values and behavior that are necessary to preserve and protect families.

It's not only the entertainment media that sucks away our time and influences our values, it's the news media as well. "Staying informed" takes up big chunks of our day, and far from being values-neutral, much of the data that reaches us is slanted, or spun, to make almost everything else seem more important than family.

Never before have we been so in touch, so well informed, so up-to-date on so much of what is going on in the world. But in addition to not being very practically useful, much of the information of our informative age is antifamily in various ways.

It is a generally accepted fact that the press and news media, taken in aggregate, is more liberal in both its ideology and its lifestyle than the average American. And the most visible conservatives in the media are often so strident and self-righteous in their style that they become hard to identify with. Thus antifamily lifestyles are treated as legitimate lifestyle alternatives and traditional, measurably functional families are portrayed as outdated, old-fashioned, or more and more often, nonexistent.

Even the "reputable" news shows seem compelled to go for what shocks us rather than for what helps us.

A personal example: 20/20 called us to ask if we'd help them with a show on values. We were excited to do so in light of some work we were doing with inner-city kids based on our Teaching Your Children Values *book. They came and filmed for two days and got some very touching footage of disadvantaged kids who were really turning their lives around by understanding and implementing honesty and courage. In one particular segment on having the courage to stand up for what you believe, a beautiful but victimized eight-year-old was responding to "scenarios" in a color-coded teaching game. "Someone offers you drugs": Yellow—"You take them"; Orange—"You say no"; Red—"You turn in the kid that offered them." None of the scenarios was hypothetical to this little girl—she'd faced them all. At the end of the game, I asked her what she thought she was: yellow, orange, or red. With a tear in her eye she said, "I've been mostly yellow, but I'm trying to hang out with more reds so I think I'm kind of orange now." It was a beautiful, positive moment—and the film crew recorded dozens more like it. But when the show was produced and aired, the upbeat, hopeful stuff was all cut. They used footage of hard, defiant kids who made shocking statements about their lack of values. Completely unbalanced, the show implied that all kids are basically monsters.*

Why is disproportionate news coverage given to violence and cruelty? Why do magazine shows and news features seem almost as preoccupied with deviance and dysfunctionality as the talk shows are? The answer, of course, has to do with profit. News ratings, just like entertainment ratings, go up in proportion to sex and violence.

The omnipresence of news and entertainment media brings things into our homes that have never been admitted before: violence on the evening news, pornography on cable, divorce statistics that are skewed to make it appear that no marriage survives, celebrities who are negative role models for our children, and a general impression that people with money and power are the ones to emulate, not the people with families.

One part of parenting that has always been assumed, if not guaranteed, is the responsibility and the opportunity of deciding *what* children should learn or be exposed to or become familiar with, *when* they should receive it, and *how* they should view it or prioritize it or think about it. Parents, in other words, were essentially in charge of how their children would initially see the world. They were thus able to mold and shape children's paradigms and early values, giving them a foundation on which to build their own beliefs and perspectives, their own lives.

The massive news and information institutions of today have seized that function—snatched it away from parents by their very pervasiveness. Short of living somewhere on a primitive island, families have no way of shielding children or screening what they see and hear.

5. Information and Communication Institutions

A generation ago, parents complained about TV—what was on it and how much time it took. But the TV was usually in the living room and it was possible to sit down with the kids and watch it. Today, the Internet poses a far more difficult challenge. Kids can go online from almost anywhere and get far more raw and explicit sex and violence than they can on TV. And much of what they can find is interactive and thus far more involving and influential. If kids want to interact with their voice rather than a keyboard and with a live person rather than images on a screen, they can call one of the 900 numbers they see advertised everywhere.

Few would want to do without the marvels of our information age. Our data and communication systems serve us magnificently. They keep us in touch, with one another and with the world. They put limitless information and knowledge at our fingertips. They tend to increase our tolerance and understanding, to break down barriers of ignorance and prejudice. Communication and information institutions—from huge telecommunications utilities to Internet companies to computer networks and systems— literally make the world work, and they make our own individual worlds so much bigger.

Nevertheless, these institutions are definite culprits in the destruction of our families. Their methods of destruction range from the relatively benign to the malignant—from the domination and consumption of our time to the intentional pollution and perversion of our children's perspectives, morality, and standards. It's a question both of how much interaction and family time a child is missing by spending five hours a day in front of a monitor and a keyboard or on the phone—of how much garbage he is ingesting from these sources.

If a parental vote could be taken, it's likely that the Internet would win out as the most feared large institution of all. With a few strokes on a keyboard—something as simple as entering the most violent and sexual words they know—kids can be in direct (and interactive) touch with hard-core pornography, with violent blood-gushing games, with online pedophiles, or with detailed instructions for how to construct a bomb. What they can get verbally over the phone lines by simply dialing a 900 number is almost as bad.

6. Political and Governmental Institutions

There have always been governments—from tribal councils to despot kings—and they have always had the power and potential to be destructive to family life. But it is only in the past several decades that the public sector, our governmental structures, has become big enough and institutionalized enough to systematically take over many of the functions of families and to monitor and tax families to the extent of threatening their viability.

The size of government today, and its scope of services, taxes families to the point of threatening their economic survival, and then it makes families seem redundant by attempting to supply, via its larger institutions, the services, the welfare, the child and elderly care, and a host of other elements that families used to provide for themselves.

Remember that on our diagram (pages 44 and 46), the public sector is the outer ring, existing for the express purpose of *protecting* the freedom and autonomy of the institutions inside (the family, the private sector, and the voluntary sector).

Unfortunately, government on virtually every level has strayed from and gone beyond that ideal, passing and implementing all kinds of obtrusive and intrusive tax and regulatory laws that undermine the inner sectors in numerous ways and that particularly threaten the bull's-eye of the family. Various branches of federal and state governments, often in well-intentioned efforts to protect individual rights, have failed to consider family rights or parental responsibilities.

Protect is the operative word, and the concept around which debate must center. *The goal must be to protect individual rights without jeopardizing families.* A tax law that makes married individuals pay more filing jointly than they would if they were single filing individually does not pass that test. Nor do laws that make it easier (and cheaper) to find day care for a newborn than to take maternity leave and nurture the child. Nor do laws that are so overzealous in protecting children that they undermine a parent's right to discipline a child, or to take him to church, or to make decisions about his education.

Our elected governments, like every large institution culprit we've identified, gravitate to their own survival and expansion and in the process overwhelm families even as they fail to protect them.

7. Educational Institutions

Ideally, schools and parents become partners in the intellectual and character education of children. In earlier days, schools were run by communities. They broadened kids' horizons and their levels of diversity and tolerance. Parents, if not in charge, at least had meaningful input and saw the schools as extensions of themselves and as helpers in bringing up their children.

Today, the massive institutions of state school systems, federal education departments, and national teachers' unions work around parents rather than through them, assuming much of the responsibility that should stay with parents and substituting (inadequately) for the family in many areas. Filled with well-meaning teachers and administrators, school systems accomplish all kinds of good things and would never identify themselves as being family-destructive in any way. Yet their *size* and *reach* can weaken families in at least four primary ways:

1. They assume responsibility for things like sex education, character education, behavior monitoring, career counseling, after-school

care, and other things that parents should be more involved in. Parents feel relieved and absolved of those responsibilities and become more removed and less communicative with their kids.

2. Schools create a school culture and a peer culture that often supersedes the family culture. Kids' time and loyalty and activity and leisure and work are all more involved with school and with various types of sports, music, dance, and other lessons than they are with family, and parents begin to think of themselves merely as the taxi service that gets them from one thing to another.

3. Schools sometimes teach antifamily or family-irrelevant views of the world. Overriding emphasis on the scientific, the economic, and the political worlds can, in the minds of children, seem to supersede the religious world or the family world.

4. Day care, preschool, and after-school programs, while providing services that many families need, can become substitutes for parents and for family time, creating situations where parents spend less and less time with children and feel less and less responsibility for them.

The ever more difficult challenge for parents is to value and appreciate all that schools can do for children but never to let the school culture or the peer culture supersede the family culture.

8. Courts and Legal Institutions

There have always been conflicts and needs for facilitators in the resolution of conflict. But large legal institutions, for whatever worthwhile purposes they serve, are inherently interested in their own preservation and growth and thus they tend to foster and even to create the very kinds of conflict that support them and keep them viable. (Illustrated by the old joke about the only lawyer in town who was starving until a second lawyer moved in and they both got rich.)

Most laws are designed for the protection of the individual, not of the family. Therefore, when two individuals try to use the law to protect their personal rights, their individual entitlement, they often proceed by pulling families apart. There are a lot more divorce lawyers than reconciliation attorneys, more custody battles than successful reuniting compromises, more probate lawyers than simple wealth transfers, more prenuptial agreements than lifetime marriages, more litigators than arbitrators, more win-lose cases than win-win scenarios.

There is no question that we need lawyers and legal institutions. But in families, we have to rely more on love and commitment than on individual rights, more on giving what is needed than on getting what we need, and more on being there for someone than on having an attorney be there for us.

Courts and the public justice system follow the same pattern as the law itself—putting the rights of individuals above the needs of family units. Courts and legal interpretations end up supporting kids who sue their parents or child protection agencies that take kids away from parents with hearsay "evidence."

Let's look separately at the family dangers imposed by our courts and by our private legal system.

A. The Courts

It's hard to imagine (and hard to overstate) the power the judicial branch of government wields through its interpretation of laws. When a judge writes an opinion, he is taking a law and telling us not only how to interpret it but how to enforce it. Thus an antifamily or family-weakening idea (or idea proponent) doesn't have to get elected to implement a destructive policy. He doesn't even have to influence the elective process or the legislature or city hall. All he or it (the person or the idea) has to do is to directly or indirectly influence an opinion written by a judge.

Here's an example: The United Nations holds a conference on families in Budapest where unbinding, theoretical resolutions are passed which point in the direction of easier divorce laws, less restrictive abortion policies, and overblown concern about population control. The delegates to this conference are not elected or even appointed. They are just self-selected people who have various political agendas. No effort has been made to balance the conference or make it representative. The resolutions are not laws or even proposals for legislation. But they go out, under a

United Nations letterhead, and begin to influence judges and legislators in this country as well as in other countries.

B. Our Private Litigation System

Litigation in general and in most of its forms is harmful to families. Typically, the only family one could argue it helps is the family of the lawyer who collects the fees. And when litigation (or custody or any other legal controversy) is between family members, it almost always tears apart and destroys relationships. It is rarely win-win. It is sometimes win-lose. It is usually lose-lose.

The whole adversarial mentality of the divorce court and litigation institution spills over into families, where spouses threaten separation rather than communicating with compromise or where family members "fight it out" as prequels to court battles rather than hashing things out in good faith and in private.

This is an area where we can learn much from the Asian mindset. Most Asian countries have less than 10 percent of the lawyers (and litigation) per capita that we do. Many have more registered arbitrators or conciliators than they do litigating or divorce lawyers.

9. Community Recreation and Social/Cultural Institutions

Recreation and social activities used to happen within and among families. Now they happen more within larger sports, music, cultural, social, and leisure institutions independent of and at the expense of families. A list of the social, cultural, and recreational institutions that have come into being during the last several decades includes everything from sports leagues to summer camps, from concert and theater guilds to fraternities, from spas and gyms to malls and fast-food restaurants. Useful as they all are, they often substitute for family time, and many create competition rather than cooperation among and between family members. Families may go together to them, but all too often these teams, clubs, guilds, camps, and societies become the identity or self-image or pride of individuals more than do their own families, and in this sense they become substitutes for family and pull away our allegiance and our attention as well as our time.

Many of these recreational, social, and cultural things happen during hours that traditionally have been family time. Evenings, weekends, summer vacations—the time blocks that families used to spend together—are now increasingly devoted to these other activities and other groups. Instead of rushing from work to home, we rush from work to bowling leagues or to the spa or to the concert or to the bridge club. Instead of having a family dinner, we refuel on the run at McDonald's. Instead of church and a family gathering on Sunday, we do the soccer league and the flute camp and then watch the big game on TV (the big games are always on Sunday).

Many parents consider the games and the camps and the clubs as their family time. They are with their kids, taking them places, watching them. But these are poor substitutes for the old traditional kinds of family time. There is little interaction between and about family members. Attention is focused on competition and comparing rather than on cooperation and communication, and the logistics and expenses of getting to everything, outfitting for everything, paying for everything create their share of stress and family tensions.

Few of us would like to do away with the recreational and social opportunities that these elements of society give us, but almost all parents, when they think about it, recognize the need to limit and govern and think about their families' involvement and the trade-offs and sacrifices that are involved.

10. Psychological and Self-Help Institutions (and the Decline—and Replacement—of Religious Institutions)

One of the more subtle and yet dangerously powerful transitions of the past century is the substitution of psychological and self-help approaches for religious institutions and approaches of faith.

Most Americans still profess belief in God and have some connection to a church, synagogue, or mosque, but more and more are inclined to turn to self-help and psychological help in dealing with their fears and problems as well as their hopes and dreams. Even the word *spiritual* has come to have more connection to self than to God. Words like *spirit, soul,* and *faith,* once the domain of religion, are trendy and popular now and often mean *my* spirit, *my* soul, *my* inner consciousness, *my* faith in *myself.* As such, they create a dependence on and reverence for self that can work against a reverence for God and a dependency on His will and power. With the self-orientation and self-help can come a kind of selfishness that detracts from family commitments and family-oriented priorities and solutions.

Most of the self-help books that line the large self-help sections of bookstores deal with three themes:

A.   Gaining more *control.*

B.   Obtaining more *ownership.*

C.   Becoming more *independent.*

While all three qualities are important and desirable in certain contexts, each one, carried to extremes or pursued too vigorously or too exclusively, can rob us of joy and faith and can seriously undermine our families because:

A. A person with true faith would give *control* to God and would not place his own importance or control above that of another person. He or she would be more interested in guidance (seeing and conforming to God's will) than in control (making things happen according to his own will). A guidance mentality makes parents more nurturing and observant and less overbearing and demanding.

B. A person with true faith would acknowledge God's *ownership* of all things and perceive himself as a steward over what God had entrusted to him. Thus he would be less materialistic and less inclined to spend all his time chasing possessions and position. In this stewardship mode, children, spouse, and family become our respected responsibilities rather than our possessions.

C. A person with true faith realizes his *dependence* on God and is more inclined to be humble and to work with others since he understands that everyone is linked and thus that we all need one another. Such persons make better—and more committed—spouses and parents than those who perceive themselves as independent islands who need no one but themselves.

As the institutions of self-help have grown and as the curses of selfishness have multiplied (teen pregnancy, violence, substance abuse, and other social problems), most religious institutions have been too silent, or too insular, or too cautious to take strong stands and make a stronger case for family priorities and family-prioritized lifestyles. There are too many politically correct religious institutions and too many religious leaders and religious teachers who emphasize tolerance at the expense of all other values and teach us that how you live doesn't matter much as long as you accept how every other person has chosen to live.

The challenge for parents is to realize how dependent they really are, how far their own skills and insights fall short, and how much they need God's help to raise God's children.

Summary of Problem Two

Ten sets of large institutions. Each born, developed, and matured during the last century to serve and sustain and make life more comfortable and convenient for individuals and families—but each evolving and mutating in ways that seriously threaten the ongoing viability of families.

As parents, we need to learn to recognize them for what they are and what they do—the good and the bad. We need to see clearly what is happening as we look out at the problem through the middle panel of our window on today's world.

LARGE NEW
INSTITUTIONS
Are Replacing Family
Institutions and
Undermining the Next
Five Essential Elements:

5. Family RULES and
   Standards
6. Family ECONOMY
   and Responsibility
   Sharing
7. Family TRADITIONS
8. Family Heritage
   and ROOTS
9. Accurate
   UNDERSTANDING
   of the Family and
   the World.

The Ballesteros family (the B family case study in the opening) is an illustration of how vulnerable families are, and how affected they can be by the influences of larger institutions. Remember how much they relied on "experts," self-help, and the technology of the broader society? Neither they nor the Calders really had time to make their families into solid, lasting institutions, with rules, traditions, roots, and an economy—because they were too involved in (and influenced by) the larger institutions that surrounded them.

Proliferating False Paradigms

and Antivalues

Why don't we, as parents, have greater resistance to the work-oriented lifestyles and materialistic priorities that are such a threat to our families? And to the undermining influences of larger institutions?

Despite the power and self-interest of the three outer rings, the family should be able to resist their destructive influences. After all, the natural bonds and self-preservation instincts of families are strong, and parents ought to be able to avoid or counter or repel the destructive influences of larger institutions and the drift toward lifestyles that are harmful to families.

So why do we parents just let it happen? Because we don't fully see the danger! We don't see our new world and its family-destructive forces accurately. Our perspectives, our world views, our paradigms have been altered by the messages we receive from the very large institutions that threaten us.

If a paradigm—or the way we see something—is off, or skewed, or blurred, then we have a false perception of reality and we can fail to see a danger or fail to see our own power or ability to solve a problem or resist a threat. For example, if media convinces us that all teenage kids get involved in early, recreational sex, we may give up on trying to help our own kids avoid it. Or if advertising converts us to the paradigm that we need a bigger house or newer car more than we need time with our kids, we may spend our time and effort on the wrong things.

Paradigm Shifts

A nearsighted child puts on glasses for the first time and sees a whole new world. A hologram shifts in the light and reveals a completely different picture. An Australian aborigine returns from a walkabout, and unaware of appendectomy, assumes evil intent from the recently arrived medical missionary whom he finds cutting his wife with a knife. The American public cheers the exposure of communist sympathizers until McCarthyism is exposed as a witch hunt. The United States ignores Nazism as an insignificant new German party until we see Hitler's goal of world domination and his massacre of Jews.

When light or insight suddenly reveals recently obscure reality, the world can suddenly look very different. Light can become dark, bad can change to good, whole world views or paradigms can shift.

Paradigms are more than perceptions. A paradigm is like a framework, a formula, an equation. When it changes, conclusions change, circumstances change, consciousness changes. *Paradigm* is a heavy word—it sounds ponderous, and it is. A paradigm shift is like an earthquake. A crust of earth slips, the old crumbles, everything is altered.

People are not as careful with their paradigms as they should be. We let our world views be manipulated by media. We let advertising persuade us of what we need. We let spin doctors style our sense of what someone said, or meant, or did.

Paradigms are powerful (and dangerous) because they are starting points. If they are unclear or inaccurate, our conclusions, our decisions, even our convictions will be inaccurate as well. Incorrect and potentially dangerous paradigms are sometimes born of simple ignorance or incomplete, lazy thinking. But they are sometimes skillfully implanted in us by those pursuing profit and power, or the simple company that misery always seeks.

Procuring, perfecting, and proclaiming proper paradigms is a little like planting a new lawn. First, root out the bad grass wherever it lies—violently, completely move it off the earth. Recognize it by holding alongside the good grass just bought. Then implant the new, nurture the good genuine green of things as they really are.

A paradigm is like a filter on a lens—it colors and alters everything we see. A paradigm is like the map of a territory. If the map is inaccurate, no amount of energy or tenacity can get us to where we want to go.

The biblical metaphor for a paradigm was old bottles which exploded when filled with new wine. If we have old-bottle paradigms, if we see the world and ourselves inaccurately, we can't handle new information well; we're less confident and sure of our convictions and our abilities; and there is stress, a desperation, and a fear of "mental explosion" as we try to cope with it all.

For example, think about the false paradigm of bloodletting. Since the problem (or the cause of people's health problems) was thought to be bad blood, bleeding, or bloodletting, was the widely accepted "cure."

What happened when it didn't work (but the false paradigm was still in place, not challenged, not replaced)? Well, better techniques were proposed—faster, better methods of bloodletting, or more of it. Better-trained bloodletters, perhaps, or better preparation and education of patients, or more money spent on bloodletting facilities. Maybe they re-engineered or restructured how they did it. Imagine PMA training for bloodletters so they could radiate positive energy or team-building or total-quality-management practices.

But of course nothing helped, because the bloodletting paradigm was wrong. In the meantime, there were clues suggesting some error in the prevailing medical cause-and-effect thinking. In war, more men were dying behind the lines in clinics than at the battle front itself. Infant mortality was better when midwives delivered than when doctors did, because midwives were cleaner.

When Anton van Leeuwenhoek discovered germs (the Dutchman called them the "wee beasties"), the paradigm changed, and everything changed with it—causes, effects, prevention. Everything shifted. Progress became possible. The problem wasn't with the blood, and the core solution wasn't even in the hospitals. The solution was back in people's personal lives— cleanliness in homes, in personal habits.

As the name implies, social problems are usually thought of as the product of society, and fixable by society. Therefore, we try to eliminate bad society with tougher laws, or more police, or bigger jails—or we try to fix society with more education or more welfare. Thinking society is the source of our social problems is like thinking bad blood was the cause of all illnesses in the nineteenth century.

In fact, until the causes—the "germ" of family breakup and negative values—are identified as the source, and the home and family are recognized as the place where change and revaluing must occur, we will be fighting the wrong battle on the wrong battlefield.

We must learn to think of the large institutions of the three outer rings and the materialistic lifestyles they set a high priority on as the bacteria that cause the illness of family breakdown, which in turn brings the pain and symptoms of serious social problems. Then, in that model, false paradigms could be thought of as an immune system deficiency that renders families unable to fight off family destruction and disintegration.

There are five key false paradigms that keep parents from seeing what is really happening to their families and that stop us from recognizing what we need to do to cure our families:

1. The Paradigm Problem of Believing That the Traditional Functions of Families Can Be Assumed and Carried Out by Other Entities

Trying to define *family* can be a tricky proposition. It's a widely used word and can mean different things to different people. The most useful approach is to define the family in terms of its essential and indispensable functions within society. Indeed, families have always played at least five critical societal roles that nothing else can fully or adequately perform.

1. The role of *procreation* and reproduction (replenishing the population).

2. The role of *nurturing* (facilitating children's emotional growth and helping them develop into responsible adults).

3. The role of providing a lasting *identity* (something permanent as everything else changes—jobs, locations, etc.).

4. The role of instilling *values* (other institutions may help, but the buck stops with the family, where values are applied as well as taught).

5. The role of offering joy and *fulfillment* to individuals (at a level beyond what is obtainable elsewhere). Children can receive a kind of unconditional and even irrational love within families that is unavailable elsewhere, and parents are refined and completed as persons through the selfless love they give to their children.

Until lately, two facts have been universally accepted: First, society cannot survive, let alone prosper, without these five functions. Second, no entity other than family can perform them adequately. These five roles or functions are an incomparable contribution to society and can be thought of as the core purposes of family and as the measurements of a family's success. When they are removed or performed by someone else, parents begin to lose their sense of purpose, and they also lose a sense of satisfaction that is available nowhere else. When parents fail to provide the five critical roles, families fade in significance, children lose identity and security, and society loses its warmth and intimacy. When our lifestyles and our priorities turn us away from the five purposes of families, our happiness and that of our children hang in the balance.

Yet today a growing, expanding paradigm suggests that perhaps we sometimes *don't* need these five functions at all, and that when we do, perhaps they *can* be performed by some entity rather than a family.

It's not that other entities can't *try* to provide these functions or play these roles for children, it's just that they can never succeed. Procreation can be performed or initiated in petri dishes and by other artificial means. Nurturing can come more and more from preschools and care providers. Identity can be gained through a club or a company or a gang. Values can be taught by media and by peer groups. Fulfillment can be gained by work. But when these needs are principally filled by entities other than family, we all lose. We lose emotionally and we lose spiritually.

Dangerous Spinoff Notions from Paradigm 1:

1. "Designer" babies and cloning

2. Intentional no-child families to allow more freedom

3. Excessive day care and ever-increasing work hours

4. Fewer family traditions and less permanence

5. Expediency over morality

6. Career given a higher priority than family

7. Children raised in groups rather than as individuals.

2. The Paradigm Problem of a Media Minority Masquerading as a Majority

We consume an enormous amount of media. Entertainment media (from music to movies to television) fills several hours each day for most Americans. We are exposed to hundreds of advertising impressions each day. And we soak in news and information constantly from radio, TV, print, and the Internet. Media literally surrounds us and permeates us.

Most entertainment media represents itself as the reflection of typical or majority lifestyles, values, and conduct. And news media poses as the reporter and revealer of events, trends, and opinions.

In fact, however, media is more and more in the business of creating trends, suggesting lifestyles, and remaking values and moral codes.

Media has given a tiny and grossly nonrepresentative minority an enormously disproportionate influence over the rest of us. In entertainment, two or three hundred individuals (media executives, producers, directors, moguls) influence virtually every movie or sit-com we see. Similar disproportionate influence exists in the music we hear. And this tiny "cultural elite" is widely removed from the American mainstream. Most are far less oriented to family and considerably less likely to be married, to attend church, or to profess belief in God. They have far more money than typical Americans. Most live jet-set, materialistically oriented lives, and they often disdain and belittle traditional values. Yet they *portray* what they produce as typical, as average, as mainstream. And they do it convincingly enough that:

- A Midwestern husband and father watches TV each night and begins to think of himself as a boring, old-fashioned dinosaur—one of the few who hasn't separated or divorced, doesn't have affairs, and actually likes to hang out at home.

- A southern housewife watches the soaps and decides (at least subconsciously) that her life is incredibly drab and unexciting and that she must be the only woman in America who stays home with young children.

- A California teenager listens to rap, goes to movies, and feels increasingly uncomfortable and out of step in being a virgin and not using drugs or alcohol. The paradigm problem is also a blockade for her parents, who see their hopes for her continuing abstinence from drugs, alcohol, and promiscuous sex as naive and unrealistic.

- A New England professional man doesn't want to be out of step or behind the trends, so he buys cars and clothes he can't afford to meet the expectations put on him by advertising.

- A grandmother in the Southwest becomes both increasingly scared of and increasingly desensitized to the violence that the media shows her to be the norm nearly everywhere. There don't seem to be many quiet, peace-loving people like herself anymore.

In reality, these people are the majority. Most Americans put a high priority on family and relationships, have faith in God and traditional values, believe in and practice fidelity in marriage, encourage chastity before marriage, avoid drugs, try to live pretty much within their means, and abhor violence and gangs. They even believe in and try to practice discipline, self-reliance, and delayed rewards, and try to avoid excessive materialism and self-gratification. They would rather see a movie about loyalty or dedication or the might of right than one about violence, debauchery, or evil. Most of us know that what we see in the media is not a morally accurate reflection, yet we are still influenced by it. In a *New York Times* poll, 46 percent said what they saw on TV was "less moral" than what really happens, and only nine percent said it was "more moral."[21]

Whenever a minority masquerades as a majority, the real majority is made to feel like a minority. Too many of us in America have been made to feel awkward and defensive about our lifestyles, about our values, about our morality. It is not only the entertainment media that is involved in this deceptive masquerade. Predominantly liberal decision makers dominate our news media—and they are not only politically liberal but morally liberal as well. Too often amoral beliefs and behavior are reported and depicted as mainstream or normal, and moral, conservative, values-driven beliefs and behavior are treated as fringe.

Statistics are constantly interpreted by much of our media as evidence of a "new morality," and the message is a subtle justification of irresponsible and amoral personal behavior. Nowhere is this more prominent than in the family-undermining statistics we read that suggest the "doomed" nature of most marriages and the near-impossible costs and obligations associated with having and raising a child. Half of all marriages, we read, end in divorce—and it will cost about $300,000 to raise and educate a child. *USA Today* says it costs over $160,000 just to raise a child through high school, with no college or education costs included.[22] And we're reminded daily of the ever-increasing numbers of children who have serious troubles with drugs, gangs, teen pregnancy, school dropout, suicide. We read it and hear it and watch it broadcast until it seems that the only safe course, the only logical decision, is to steer clear of the land mines of marriage, family, and children.

In fact, there is huge misinterpretation of statistics. There was *one* year in which there were half as many divorces in America as there were marriages, but there are far more married adults than single ones. So the numbers do not mean that half of the marriages are ending in divorce. In fact, over 80 percent of first marriages survive until death. Nearly 85 percent of married people are still married to their original marriage partner. And 90 percent of unmarried adults say they want to be married and plan to be married.

And statistics actually show that adults with children do better financially than those without. Of course children cost money, but they can also help and earn and become independent. And while it is hard to raise kids today, and many families are in trouble, it is, of course, still possible to create strong families and raise successful children.

What a tragedy it is when a false paradigm keeps people from life's most joy-providing experiences and roles and stewardships—those of marriage, commitments, children, and family.

As though it weren't enough to have such a small and untypical minority exerting such a huge influence through the mainstream media, the paradigm problem is further exacerbated by the fact that many of the things most of us do believe in are being championed in media by people who seem either so self-righteous or so little like us that we have a hard time identifying with them.

> A friend recently said, "The people I cannot stand to watch or listen to are television evangelists and right-wing radio and TV commentators."
>
> "You don't like what they're saying?" I asked.
>
> "I don't even know what they're saying," she answered. "They are just so shrill and so self-righteous . . . and either so abrasive or so syrupy smooth that I just can't stand them."

Why is it that the conservative, values-oriented, family-centered, God-acknowledging message most of us agree with is so often delivered or represented by people with personalities that polarize, by people with whom many can't identify—egocentrics, extremists, even bigots? And why, on the other hand, are so many of the liberal, politically correct, and often anti-family-and-values messages presented so appealingly by such appealing people?

The bottom-line danger of the first false paradigm is this: When we perceive things around us to be worse, less moral, and less hopeful than they really are, we tend to give up, to cave in, to think, "If you can't beat them, join them." It's the old ad-man gimmick of "everyone's doing it, so why not you?" The false paradigm grows far beyond a simple misperception. We laugh and join in and think we must be on the right train because everyone else is there. But we're headed for a cliff.

Dangerous Spinoff Notions from False Paradigm 2:

1. "Everybody does it" (especially casual, recreational sex).

2. Violence is just part of the landscape and shouldn't shock or disturb us that much.

3. "Tolerance is the prime virtue—anything that anyone does is okay."

4. "Traditional values and traditional families are out-of-date and old-fashioned."

5. "There are no consequences."

6. "You're in touch, therefore in tune."

7. "We don't create society's values, we just reflect them."

Someone has said, "Like earlier generations, we look out at the world through glass rectangles. The difference is, we turn ours on with a switch." How much does media influence us? Does it give us an accurate picture of the world? Why are we (and particularly our children) so inclined to believe what they see on the big and small screen and to identify with what they hear in the lyrics of popular music? Generally speaking, does the media work for or against the values you want to teach your children?

3. The Paradigm Problem of Emphasizing Achievements Over Relationships and of External Security Over Internal

You don't hear of people on their deathbeds saying, "Oh, if only I'd spent more time with the business." Most of our regrets and our guilt comes from inadequate efforts in our relationships—too little time with family. We acknowledge that relationships are more important than achievements, but our actions are not congruent with our beliefs.

This third paradigm problem is closely related to the second. The masquerading minority promotes materialism and encourages us to measure and judge by wealth, position, comfort, social status, ownership. But it's more than that. We live in a world where profit is the bottom line, where everything is explained in an economic model. Money (instead of being the means to worthy ends like education, family, experience, and service to others) is thought of as an end in itself.

In many cases, we gravitate to achievements because they are easier than relationships—easier to obtain, to preserve, and to measure. They are also less risky; they take less emotional energy. So we go for achievement and for ownership, even though, deep down, most of us know that the very concept of ownership (which drives most of our "achieving") is flawed. When we take the long-range perspective, we really don't own anything. Things pass through us. We are temporary stewards over everything we supposedly own, from our cars and houses to our children. An ownership mentality always produces greed, envy, and jealousy on the one hand and pride, conceit, and condescension on the other. Yet we all seem locked into the idea of wanting more.

Another aspect of this paradigm problem is thinking that our sense of inadequate safety is caused by gangs, violence, too little protection, and too few police officers—and that it can be solved by more of them. "Crime" is now a prominent answer to the public opinion survey question "What is the biggest problem in America today?" Most Americans feel insecure and vulnerable. The buffer of law and order that used to separate good, respectable citizens from the elements of violence and fear has been permeated and knocked down. So we campaign for external solutions—more police enforcing more laws, bigger prisons, and tougher drug penalties. We make our kids paranoid about strangers, and we arm ourselves with guns and Mace, and still we can't recover the feeling of safety.

In fact, the crime problem is caused by the breakdown of the families and will be solved only by the revaluing of families and the inner recommitment to values. Kids join gangs because they need a larger-than-self identity and security that they don't find in their dysfunctional and inadequate homes. People use drugs to escape the reality of crumbling or nonexistent relationships. And violence erupts out of the frustration of wrong expectations and failure at the things that really matter.

The error of worldly paradigms and of placing too high a priority on external achievements, wealth, or security is *always* exposed in personal life, as individuals achieve these external things and still find no inner peace or deep satisfaction. But we need to acknowledge it before we spend a lifetime figuring it out. We need to reject it early rather than later, while our lives (and the real joys) are still ahead of us.

Dangers Spinoff Notions from False Paradigm 3:
1. "You are your work."
2. "He who dies with the most toys wins."
3. "Image is everything."
4. "All I want is the land next to mine."
5. "It takes at least two full-time incomes to raise a family."
6. "You deserve it before you earn it (instant gratification)."
7. "Have it all."
8. "More is better."
9. "It's impossibly expensive to raise a child."
10. "Money is the goal. Work is our identity. Economics is the explanation."

4. The Paradigm Problem of Recreational Sex, Hedonism, and Instant Gratification

Our society somehow manages to glorify and debase sex at the same time—both falsely. Sex is portrayed and perceived as the ultimate pleasure, the ultimate test of manhood or womanhood, the almost instant result (and gratification) of any romantic encounter. Alternatively, it is portrayed and perceived as cheap, casual, or violent.

This false paradigm tells us that fidelity is rare in marriage and that chastity is almost nonexistent prior to marriage. It implies that singles and swingers have more sex (and enjoy it more) than people who are monogamous and married. Furthermore, the paradigm implies that marriage is boring, spells the end of romance, and causes two people to take each other for granted.

In reality (in the true paradigm), things are very different. Over 80 percent of married women and nearly as high a percentage of married men have never had an extramarital affair. More than half of female high school graduates are virgins. Married adults report more and better sex than unmarried "swingers" (more quantity and quality). Marriage, when it is worked at and committed to, brings the peace and security we all long for and can produce a miraculous kind of synergy where two people become more than the sum of their parts. And romance of the mind and spirit—courtship that saves the physical union until the time of commitment and marriage—still exists, still works, still *thrives*. And the point is, it would thrive more and produce more joy for us all if we could rid ourselves of the false paradigm.

A connected paradigm problem is that personal discipline and conservative values are perceived as constraints and freedom inhibitors.

> *A former business partner of ours used to say, "If it feels good, do it." He prided himself in living for the moment, having it now, and holding no inhibitions.*
>
> *Because of our association with him, we were particularly aware of how often his philosophy was reinforced by the media and by the prevailing attitudes around us. We noticed how frequently ministers or preachers were portrayed on TV or in the movies as out-of-touch, uptight fuddy-duddies, or as hypocrites—how often the heroes were wild rebels, liberal carousers, or big-hearted whores.*

Too often in this paradigm, nice guys finish last—or are not even in the race. People live or behave irresponsibly, without consequences. And standards, from religious commandments to committed personal values, are seen as chains that tie people down and take away their freedom to act, to express themselves, to live fully.

Actually, of course, the precise opposite is true. Irresponsibility and instant gratification always have their consequences, and immoral and amoral behavior always hurts people—and ultimately hurts its practitioner. And the consequences and the hurts are what rob people of the freedom to live fully and to find their best selves.

The fundamental problem with the false paradigm of hedonism is that it is a lie and it actually takes from us the very freedom that it promises to give.

Perhaps the essential difference between humans and animals is that animals achieve their purpose and potential by following and being controlled by their instincts and appetites. People, on the other hand, achieve their full purpose and highest potential by controlling and governing their appetites. Whether the appetite is for food, sex, power, wealth, or achievement, happiness comes through control and discipline.

Spiritually, inwardly, we know this is true, yet it is so much easier to let the appetite win. And in today's false paradigm, appetite is tied to excitement and fulfillment and instant rewards keep reinforcing the immoral behavior, while values (which are essentially appetite controls) are thought of as boring and old-fashioned.

Dangerous Spinoff Notions from False Paradigm 4:
1. "What I do in my private life affects only me."
2. "If it feels good, do it."
3. "Nice guys finish last."
4. "Affairs are the norm; teen sex is the norm."
5. "Sex is recreation."
6. "You owe yourself."

5. The Paradigm Problem of Conditional or Situational Ethics and Relying on the "Reality" of the Physical, the Practical, the Psychological, and the Philosophical Rather than the Spiritual

Conditional ethics, values-neutral education, and a host of other confusing and pain-producing notions spring from our efforts to explain and deal with our world without acknowledging inherent good or evil.

And while it may not be politically correct to reference belief in God or in the devil, most Americans do believe in both. The experience of the ages and the logic of our minds tell us that certain core values—honesty, peacefulness, courage, loyalty, responsibility, fidelity, respect, self-discipline, self-reliance, love, mercy, basic kindness—are essential to the survival of a society and of its essential institutions, down to and including the family.

While we were writing our book Teaching Your Children Values, *we were confronted more than once by media interviewers who demanded, "Well, whose values is your book going to advocate?" The implication was that there is some huge pot full of values and each of us selects our own by individual preference. We had answers to these questions because we'd done our homework. As we wrote the book, we solicited input from large numbers of parents with diverse backgrounds from all over the world. The bottom line is simple: Virtually all people share certain basic and universal values and want those values to be embraced by their children.*

The essence of this fourth paradigm problem is that while almost everyone pays lip service to certain basic values, we *apply* them selectively and sporadically—and our larger institutions often encourage their compromise. For example:

- Easy credit undermines self-discipline.
- Erratic welfare systems erode self-reliance.
- Merchandising/advertising downplay balance and delayed gratification.
- Complex tax codes encourage dishonesty.
- Macho attitudes and media violence contradict peaceableness.
- Media- and merchandising-induced trends and peer pressure undermine kids' courage to be themselves and follow their own standards.
- Loyalty to family is replaced by economically mandated loyalty to job.
- Respect and unselfishness are replaced by the exploitation and expediency it takes to get ahead.
- Kindness and friendliness are knocked out of us by suspicion and fear.
- Media amorality and the glamorization of stereotypes of recreational sex discourage fidelity and chastity.
- Self-help and pop psychology emphasize self-fulfillment and revenge at the expense of love and mercy.

As the stress and complexity of daily life have increased over the past half century, the two recurring "solutions" thrown at us by our pop culture and our self-help writers and speakers have been: (1) positive mental attitude and (2) time management. "You can do anything," goes the positive-mental-attitude thesis. "Every day in every way you are getting better and better!" "Whether you think you can or think you can't, you're right!" "Whatever the mind of man can conceive and believe, it can achieve." The time-management solution tells us to plan everything, control everything, "act, don't react." "Never be surprised." "Live by your list." Both positive-attitude and time-management ideas are comforting—and motivating—but neither one is completely true, and in the long run, both set us up for a fall. The fact is that we *can't* do everything. We're actually pretty limited in what we can do on our own. And— sorry—we just don't get better every day in every way. As much as we might like to control everything, plan everything, and never be surprised, life doesn't work that way. The only truly predictable thing is unpredictability.

In fact, our human inadequacies can make us humble, faith-filled, and ultimately powerful through a higher power. And the surprises, opportunities, and unplannable, spontaneous serendipities are what make life interesting and entertaining. Family life, especially, doesn't work in a predictable, scheduled, always positive way. When a child needs help or has a question at an inconvenient moment, we can't "pencil him in" on another day. Families have ups and downs; they test the extremes of our emotions in both directions.

This paradigm problem of "self-help" is more than a matter of applying the wrong techniques. It is a problem of false realities. When we think of the spiritual as less real than the physical, of impressions as less reliable than sensory evidence, of guidance and inspiration as something exclusive to monks or gurus, of spirituality as a less important "science" than psychology or philosophy—when we make these paradigm mistakes, we give up what is most real within us. As Pierre Teilhard de Chardin said, "We are not human beings having a spiritual experience, we are spiritual beings having a human experience."

Trying to explain everything physically and empirically is actually a phenomenon of just the past couple of centuries. Before that, most perspectives and explanations were spiritual. In the Renaissance, science and a revival of the arts became temporal alternatives to excessive religious power and unsatisfying, simplistic spiritual explanations. Today, more and more of us see the inadequacy and shallowness of the secular, scientific explanation, and we look ever deeper at the spiritual.

Very few of us, deep down, want to be a "material girl" or a material guy. Our desires are spiritual and our finest hours often come in the enlightenment and courage of faith rather than in the limited and fearful insistence on self-reliance.

Ultimately, *self-help* (in the psychological or the scientific sense) is an oxymoron. We can work to be our best, because we hold within us powers of self-improvement. But to truly lift to another level, to go beyond our very finite and limited abilities, to see realities that are beyond our senses, for these we need non-self-help. We need help from a higher source, from a spiritual source, from God.

Simply acknowledging this, simply releasing the false paradigm of one-dimensional self-help, liberates us and lifts a weight from our heads. It is less empowering to say, "I can do anything," than to say, "I can do very little by myself, but I have faith in a higher, stronger, better power that can guide and illuminate and help."

Dangerous Spinoff Notions from False Paradigm 5:
1. Conditional (changing) ethics.

2. "Values-neutral education."

3. Poverty causes the destruction of values (rather than the reverse).

4. "I can do anything I want and have anything I want."

5. "I am number one."

6. "All of my problems are emotional and mental, not spiritual."

7. "Religion is self-serving and self-righteous."

8. "We can understand and explain everything."

9. There is no ultimate source of good.

Summary of Problem Three

It could be well argued that nothing is more dangerous than a well-entrenched false paradigm. When our perspective or mental grasp of things is wrong, it allows wrong things to happen to us and to be done by us. Most of what the broader society does to families and to children happens because parents have accepted false paradigms that let destructive things happen. And the negative effects of supercharged lifestyles get out of control, because our false paradigms don't challenge them or adjust them.

The fact is, there is no such thing as a "values-neutral" curriculum or program or *situation*. Values are always there, in every peer-group conversation, on every TV show, in every environment, on every Internet site. False paradigms and antivalues are in the air, and parents will never remove them. Parents can only hope to override and replace them with correct principles and true values.

FALSE PARADIGMS AND ANTIVALUES are crowding out and choking off the final two elements of families

10. Correct PRINCIPLES
11. Basic VALUES

Most of the problems of the Calder family in the opening case studies came about not so much because of what *was* happening as because of what *wasn't* happening. Clear and solid values and principles were not being consciously or consistently taught—thus there was no offense, and the parents had to rely almost completely on defense, which often wasn't enough. The Calders, while well meaning, were pretty much blinded by false paradigms. At the other extreme, the Alder family, by making a conscious effort to teach correct principles and basic values, was countering the antivalues and false paradigms that swirled around their children.

PART II

Looking In at the Solutions

How families can succeed and prosper despite

it all—three corresponding antidote/solutions

and "the eleven essential elements

of happy families"

Looking In

We've looked out through the three-paneled window and seen the new, difficult environment of the twenty-first century. We've seen how negatively its materialistic lifestyles, large self-serving institutions, and false paradigms can impact families. The good news is that it doesn't all have to impact *our* families. The question of Part Two is What do we see as we look *in* through those same three windows—into our own homes? Can we put in place, inside our homes where our families grow, carefully conceived antidotes that counter the outside poison?

In the Opening section, on pages 22–23, we made the claim that there are eleven qualities that always exist in some form in relatively happy, functional, and succeeding families—eleven common elements that are always consciously or subconsciously there. These elements are the perfect antidotes to the problems outlined in Part One. They counter, neutralize, and overcome these problems and stimulate strong, unified families and help parents produce children who are confident, sensitive, and secure.

Recall the window looking *in.*

Specific, well-planned	Specific, well-planned	Specific, well-planned
efforts to	efforts to	efforts to
create a serene,	build a family	teach strong values and
family-oriented	institution and	correct
lifestyle that	infrastructure	principles,
counters the	that is a	which
world's	stronger influence	overcome the antivalues
chaotic	on kids than	and
"busyness,"	larger "outside"	false
complexity, and	institutions	paradigms
materialism		of the world

As we look into our homes from the chaos and confusion of the world outside, the eleven essential elements can be viewed through the windows according to which problems they address and overcome.

Creating a family-oriented lifestyle:	Building a family institution and infrastructure:	Teaching strong values and correct principles:
1. RECOMMITMENT	5. Family RULES/Standards	9. Correct PRINCIPLES
2. PURPOSE	6. Family "ECONOMY"	10. VALUES Therapy
3. PRIORITIZING	7. Family TRADITIONS	
4. COMMUNICATIONS	8. Family Heritage and ROOTS	
	9. UNDERSTANDING the place of family and of other institutions	

As mentioned, the eleven elements don't just happen anymore (most of them did happen rather naturally in earlier generations, in times before the emergence of the hectic lifestyles, large institutions, and false paradigms that work against them today). We now have to create the elements by conscious effort and put them into place in our families with persistence and determination.

What follows here in Part Two is a guide for doing just that. It will not happen overnight. It is not a quick fix. It takes time and effort and energy, none of which busy parents have any excess of. But there is a promise that can motivate us all. It is simply this: Parents who *take* the time to establish the eleven elements will end up *saving* time in the long run. This promise will come about in two ways: First, they will save time because the eleven elements are like an infrastructure. They take time and effort to build (like a city that builds bridges, roads, and water systems), but once they are in place, the family runs smoother with less effort, and some time-consuming problems you would otherwise have to deal with never happen at all. Second, parents will save time in an even more important sense of the word. They will save or purchase time because there will be a longer span of time in which their children will trust in them, listen to them, and communicate with them. Children who come from homes where the eleven elements are present seldom become alienated from their parents. And even as they move out into their own independent spheres, they retain a positive emotional tie to their homes and to their parents throughout their lives, continuing to honor and sustain their roots and their traditions and passing on the same eleven essential elements to their own children.

Our goal here in Part Two is not only to convince you that the eleven elements are desirable and important and that they will effectively overcome the aspects of the world that work against families; we also want to convince you that you really can have them in *your* family, that they are accessible, that you can build them, that while they may take time, none of them are beyond your reach.

Create a More Family-Oriented

Lifestyle and a Planning

System That Puts a High

Priority on the Family

Solution One, designed to overcome the problem of materialistic lifestyles and wrong-turned hearts, incorporates the first four of the eleven essential elements: (1) A conscious *recommitment* to the first priority of marriage and to family and children. (2) Clear family *purpose* via a family mission statement. (3) The reinvention of *time management,* with the emphasis on spouse and children and with certain time periods set aside and reserved for family. (4) *Communication* implemented, improved, and insisted upon— between spouses and between parent and child. Together, these four elements will completely neutralize and overcome the hectic lifestyles and other misplaced priorities that can pull families apart.

These first four essential elements must each be used and adjusted according to the ages of your children, and they will work best if you tailor them to meet the unique and specific needs of your own family and situation. Revise, reconfigure, and reinvent each approach until it fits your family and until it becomes yours rather than ours. Think of everything in Part Two not as *our* thinking but as our consulting and as idea prompters to stimulate *your* thinking. You are the only expert on your family and your children!

Essential Element One: RECOMMITMENT

A good friend of ours, a country doctor who has attended the last hours of many people's lives, remarked that he had never heard anyone on their deathbed say, "Oh, I wish I'd spent more time with the business," or "If only I'd been able to buy one more new car." The regrets people have at the end of life (as well as their most cherished memories) invariably have to do with family.

The regrets come not only at the very end of life. So many in their fifties, sixties, or seventies, even those who have every material thing they ever wanted, find their lives empty and hollow, lonely and meaningless because they forfeited family somewhere along the way. They miss so desperately the relationships that they gave up (or gave up on) sometime back in midlife.

The pattern is so frighteningly predictable: In "early life" we fall in love, start families, and know the joys and sorrows that come with the risks of committed, caring relationships. In midlife we grow impatient, disillusioned, or just tired, and allow some combination of selfishness, foolishness, and fatigue to turn us away from spouse or child. Or we simply stop putting forth the necessary effort and let family relationships gradually slip and slide away. Then in late life we realize that what we gave up was everything and what we traded it for is nothing.

It is in midlife (sometimes very early midlife—this time of slippage and selfishness) that we need a purposeful and powerful recommitment to relationships. Deep down, we all know that family is the first priority and that no other success can compensate for failure in the home. Yet the world pulls us in so many other directions. The false paradigms and the self-preserving larger institutions popularize materialism, self-gratification, and the "freedom" of ownership without obligation.

Thoughts that are destructive to the family come so easily. "My wife doesn't look as good as she used to." "I just don't have the energy to keep track of this kid anymore." "My spouse is so much less stimulating than the people I work with at the office." "My life is so dull compared with what I see on TV." "Think of what I could have if I spent a little more of what I earn on myself." "Once kids are this age, there's not much I can do to influence them anyway." "I'm completely tied down by my spouse and kids." "There's got to be something more to life than this." "I'm just tired of trying to do everything for everyone else and nothing for myself." The thoughts gradually work their way into negative words and actions.

We need an antidote—a vaccination against the slippage. The pre-scription we need is *recommitment*. Real commitment—deep and heartfelt commitment—is a "root" solution. It is the essence and the core of turning our very hearts. It is a solution that moves up through the trunk and extends out to affect every branch and leaf. "Parenting methods" or "marriage techniques" may work here and there, but genuine commitment affects everything we do, and more important, everything we and those around us *feel*.

Commitment is hard to describe but easy to feel—even vicariously through a story: When I [Richard] was a young man, the church we went to had a pro-gram in which the lay members would visit the homes of other members once a month to see how they were doing and to leave a brief spiritual thought or message. I was assigned to two families, one of which was very wealthy and attractive—easy to admire. The man, about ten years older than I, had a suc-cessful business, a beautiful wife, bright kids, and a mansion of a house, and drove a Lamborghini. The second family was quite a contrast—poor, small house, seven people with only one bathroom.

I looked forward to my visit to the first family each month—so much style and stimulation. The other house was pretty routine. Yet as the months passed, I found my anticipation shifting. I looked forward to the little house because the feelings and the atmosphere were so good there. And what had seemed to be busyness and excitement at the big house was revealing itself to be tension and all kinds of conflict and dissatisfaction—everyone running off in a different direction, trying to find something fulfilling.

We moved away a year or two later and I lost touch with both families. Fifteen years later, I was giving a speech at a university, and afterward a student came up and asked if I remembered her. She was one of the children from the small and humble house. As we talked, I sensed that same comfortable, quietly confident feeling that I used to feel in their home. I asked about the other family with the big house, and she told me that the parents had broken up and a couple of the kids were in rehab programs. I asked how her family was.

"Oh, we're all fine," she said. "Still not too well off, but everyone is making progress and we love each other more than ever."

Then I asked about her father. "What did he do that gave you all such confidence?" I wondered "What were his parenting techniques? I'm a dad now and I want that same feeling in my home."

On my second question she seemed a little amused. "You remember my dad," she said. "He wouldn't know a parenting technique if it came up and bit him."

"That's true, but what did he do?" I said. "I still remember how it felt in your home and I still see it in your eyes now." She became more reflective and I saw something else in her eye—a tear. "You know," she said, "I think it was just that we knew he'd never give up on us. We knew we were his first priority. He would make mistakes—he had a temper, still does—but he was just always there for us, and he'd tell us that."

I think it was my obvious interest in what she was saying that kept her memories coming. "I remember he would come and sit on my bed and just hold my face in his hands and look right in my eyes and say, 'I am totally committed to you. You are my first priority. I may screw up and you may screw up on this or that, but I will never give up on you and I will never stop loving you completely. You can count on that! You kids and your mother are my life. No matter what, you'll always be the most important thing to me. I'm committed to your mother and I'm committed to you—always. Don't you ever forget that!' "

She hadn't ever forgotten it, and its powerful and secure effect still seemed to rest on her.

The interesting thing about marriage and parenting and family is that *no one ever fails until they give up.* There will be setbacks and problems, sometimes big, long-term problems. We see examples of that every day. We see parents who hang in there, who keep trying, keep supporting, keep giving their unconditional love, and keep *telling* their child of it—kids who are in trouble, kids who have run away, kids who won't listen, won't talk—and those kids eventually come around! Maybe not tomorrow, maybe not next year, maybe not in ten years, but when the parent never quits, reconciliation does come, improvement does come. The same commitment magic almost always works between marriage partners. Every imaginable problem may exist, but when no one throws in the towel, where the commitment is still there, things eventually get better!

The real question, of course, is how we *apply* commitment. After we profess it to those we love most, how do we demonstrate it in everyday life? The answer here—and the beauty of it, actually—is that different people will apply it in different ways. If your recommitment is real, it will manifest itself in ways that are tailored to your own situation and your family's own needs. The techniques are not as important as the heart, the methods are not as important as the commitment.

Too many parents approach the process backwards. They read of various parenting techniques and try them in hopes of increasing their feelings and their commitments. But if the heart is not there—not genuinely and truly turned to the family in a prioritized, unconditional love—then the methods will be hollow and generally ineffective.

Even having said that, there is one method we suggest to every parent—a mental method—a method for marshaling other methods, a method that is a direct manifestation of a turned heart, a method that has placed itself at the center of our marriage and our family for decades.

We call it a "Five-Facet Review," and it works like this: Once a month (it's best if there is a set day, like the first Tuesday), go on a "date" with your spouse if you are a two-parent family or with someone else who really knows and loves your children if you are a single parent. Go to dinner in a relatively quiet place where you are unlikely to be disturbed, and have only one item on your agenda—your children. Talk together about the five facets of each of your children, one at a time: How is Billy doing physically? How is he doing mentally? How is he doing socially? How is he doing emotionally? How is he doing spiritually? With each facet, think about potential problems, and also about potential opportunities or attributes. Take notes. When you recognize a challenge or a need (or an opportunity), decide how to deal with it and who will handle it. You will leave with a clearer picture of a child and a more specific commitment to him and a more sharply focused love for him. Your heart will turn. The next month, bring your notes from the previous session. How are things changing? What has been resolved? Did you follow through? Pin down the needs and focuses for next month as you go through the five facets once again.

Commitment is sometimes strengthened (and recommitment is best made) by some sort of formal process. Often just wanting to be committed or saying you'll try is not enough.

There are two ways of "formalizing a recommitment" that are especially effective:

1. *Write it down and turn it into a document that you present to each other.* The language can be simple, but the more absolute it is, the better. Use some *herebys* and *wherefores* along with your own creativity and write out a "commitment document," first to your spouse if you are married and second to your children. If you have more than one child, do a separate one (or at least a separate copy) for each.

One powerful recommitment pledge starts off something like this:

I, Craig Calder, hereby recommit myself, my resources, my gifts, and my soul to you, Cathy Calder, as my highest priority, my wife, and the only romantic love of my life. While I am far from perfect as a husband, there are many things you can absolutely and always count on from me. One is that I will put you and your interests first in every choice or decision I face. Two is that I will always be completely honest with you and have no secrets from you. Third is that I will be a full partner with you in the raising of our children. Fourth is that I will never let other priorities (work, sports, etc.) get ahead of you and the kids in my mind or cause me to do anything that would damage or impact negatively on you or on your happiness. Fifth is that I will remember and keep our marriage vows. . . .

It could go on from there. Can you imagine any wife or child who would not love and appreciate such a document—or who would not feel warmed and more secure with it?

2. *Take your family to a special place or on a special trip to verbally make your*

recommitment to them. Many families have a special place—perhaps where they go on vacation or where they have some special memory. If you have a place like this, take your family there and make a formal recommitment to them, either verbally or in writing. Build up to it, anticipate it together as a family, and take notes on it in some kind of a family journal or diary.

We tend to undervalue and underestimate commitment. We forget about its pervasive power. Real commitment, when it is felt, when it is expressed, when it is present in the air, has a way of shrinking problems, of making them look manageable. When commitment is thought of as unalterable, eternal, and unconditional, problems just can't stand up to it—they can't match it in its permanence. Whatever the forces are that undermine relationships and break up families, they tend to back off in the presence of deep, complete commitment, as though they had a mind of their own and chose to go work on someone else where there is less commitment and where they can do more damage.

Commitment is turning your heart more toward your family, locking your heart on the relationships that matter. If you want to fix our families, to shore up your children against the false paradigms and the larger institutions, to immunize them against all of their many potential destroyers, you must start with recommitment. Let the recommitment start in your heart, and then you will be capable of sending it out through your words and your eyes to reassure and bless the lives of those you love most. You will then have obtained the first essential element!

Essential Element Two: A Family Mission Statement or Declaration of PURPOSE

Every business seems to have one—on a plaque, on the wall: an attractively worded statement of vision and purpose and goals. Employees are proud of it and hope to do their part to bring it to pass.

In the Opening, we mentioned a man who carried two mission statements— in the two inside breast pockets of his suit jacket. In the right pocket was his

corporate mission statement: he was president and CEO of a highly prof-
itable mid-sized company. In the left ("over my heart," he said) was his fam-
ily mission statement.

Let us tell you how the family one came about. He told us that he and his
wife had taken their three teen and elementary-school-age children to a
resort hotel for a long weekend, rented a conference room there (I was think-
ing it would have worked just as well on a camping trip), and held several
two-hour sessions (interspersed with swimming and activities) where they
hammered out a family mission statement. He said they'd started just talk-
ing about their family, their love for one another, and their desire to stay
together and support one another, and how they could use what they had to
help others. The dad had read them some corporate mission statements and
asked if they thought one was needed in the family. At a second session they
had each written down what was most important to them and, interestingly,
a list of their favorite words. At a third session they'd each written up a sim-
ple personal mission statement—hopes and dreams for their individual lives.
At a final session they pulled everything together and created a family mis-
sion statement. They had a big framed copy at their home, and each carried
a laminated personal copy.

We were so impressed that we tried it. Here is a sampling of what we
came up with:

FIFTEEN-YEAR-OLD NOAH'S PERSONAL MISSION STATEMENT:

To be looked upon by others and by God with a smile always. To be filled with
a joy that others can feel. To find this joy through service. To watch, to absorb,
to learn, to find, to discover, to think carefully about school, career, and family
goals, and then to reach them. To always look forward to the next day.

—NOAH EYRE

A portion of our collectively written family mission statement:

Create together
an identity-building, support-giving family institution
that fosters and facilitates a maximum

of broadening and contributing by its members,
who have become strong, independent
individuals, committed spouses,
and parents beyond their parents.
First receiving and then giving the gifts
of joy, responsibility, and sensitivity
and approaching the world with attitudes of
serendipity, stewardship, and synergy.

And a piece of our parenting mission statement:

Help children to grow up and spin off into independent orbits,
still feeling the gravity and light of parents
with whom there is a consulting relationship
in which advice is freely asked for, freely given,
and used or unused without offense to parent
or pressure to child.

Our dear friend Stephen Covey has been called the father of the mission statement. He has helped countless large corporations fashion the framed missions statements we so often see on the walls of corporate headquarters around the world.

But Stephen's favorite mission statement is the one he and his wife Sandra and their children created for their family. It is beautiful in its simplicity:

The mission of our family is to create a nurturing place of order, truth, love, happiness, and relaxation, and to provide opportunities for each person to become responsibly interdependent, in order to achieve worthwhile purposes.

The process by which the Coveys created that statement is not as simple as the result. It took time, and mental effort, and lots of communication.

Stephen suggests three steps:

STEP 1: EXPLORE WHAT YOUR FAMILY IS ALL ABOUT.
Ask and discuss:

- What is the purpose of our family?

- What are we all about in life?

- What is our identity as a family?

- What kind of a family do we want? *Note: Questions 5 through 9 are geared to children.*

- What kind of a home do you want to invite friends to?

- What is embarrassing to you?

- What makes you feel comfortable at home?

- What makes you want to come home?

- What makes you feel drawn to us as parents so that you are open to our influence? How can we as parents be more open to your influence?

- What are the things that are truly important to us as a family?

- What are our family's highest-priority goals?

- What are our unique talents, gifts, and abilities?

- What are the priorities we want our family to operate on (such values as trust, honesty, kindness, service)?

STEP 2: WRITE YOUR FAMILY MISSION STATEMENT.
Five guidelines:

- Include the desired characteristics of the home and the desired effect of the mission statement on family members.

- Write it as if it were timeless.

- Deal with both ends and means.

- Deal with the four basic needs: to live, to love, to learn, to leave a legacy.

- Deal with all family roles.

STEP 3: STAY ON COURSE.

Ask yourself periodically:

- How are we living in relationship to our family mission statement and destination?
- What do we need to do to get back on course?
- How can we keep ourselves actively working on our family mission statement as our family constitution?

Any family can create a family mission statement at any phase of their lives. An engaged or soon-to-be-married couple can write one projecting how they will treat each other and their children, how they will finance their family, and what they will give high priority to. Single parents can write one that solidifies relationships and shares responsibilities with children. Blended families can write one that sets goals and guidelines for relating to married children and grandchildren. Mission statements can include approaches to caring for elderly parents or financing children's college educations.

The beauty of family mission statements is that they involve thought and prioritizing and communication. They focus family members on their positive interdependence and on their love for one another. Take the time and make the effort. It won't be easy, and your first result or first draft may not be a "keeper," but none of the time or thought spent on it is wasted, and you will eventually produce and be proud of a document representing the second essential element!

Essential Element Three: Reinvent Time Management to Prioritize with Family

It's ironic that as we've pushed goal- and priority-setting time management nearly to an art form, few of us have figured out how to make it produce any more time for our highest priority—our families. We come up with lots of "solutions" (which are really excuses), like "quality time" or pagers so our kids can reach us, or availability on our cell phones. But have you noticed that real quality time usually happens when there is an adequate, unrushed *quantity* of time. And our kids don't just need to know how to reach us when there is an emergency, they need us to be there to focus on them when there is no need other than the need for time together.

> I [Richard] remember, as a young parent, feeling absolutely swamped with responsibilities and opportunities at work, getting home after the kids were in bed and leaving the next morning before they were awake. I felt especially guilty about not spending more time with my five-year-old son, who seemed to really need a dad. Whenever he wanted something, I'd be gone or about to leave.
>
> I thought, in those days, that time management was the answer or the solution to just about everything; so I simply thumbed ahead a few pages in my day timer until I saw a free evening the next Thursday and I blocked it off for Josh. Almost immediately, I felt a little less guilty. It was down in the book! So I really wasn't neglecting him! But when Thursday came there was a minor crisis at the office and I knew I'd have to stay late. But no problem, I'd just pencil Josh in for a week from Tuesday. Since I'd wanted to surprise him, I hadn't mentioned anything to him yet, anyway. So he wouldn't know the difference. Quality time was scheduled again, so I was once again off the hook in my own mind.
>
> When Tuesday came I actually left work a few minutes early and showed up at the house right on schedule (my schedule). Josh was sitting in front of the TV when I burst in. "Come on, son, let's go do something fun together!" He looked up at me (probably trying to remember who I was) and said, "Not now, Dad. I've got to watch The Incredible Hulk."

What a mistake we make when we think we can program our kids or have them want to be with us right when it's convenient, or schedule them like a business meeting. Kids need us when they need us, and quality time comes not when we dictate but when circumstances provide us with a teaching moment—when we're spontaneous enough to answer a question or play a game or tuck a child into bed even when it's *not* convenient or written down in our day timer. This kind of occasional serendipity is a hallmark of good parents and it demonstrates to kids that they really are the first priority.

This is not to say we can't schedule some family time. Indeed, doing so may be the most important solution of all. But it needs to be scheduled *with* the kids so they can anticipate it, and plan on it, and start anticipating it and enjoying it even before it happens.

The problem with most time management is that it focuses on achievements at the expense of relationships, on work goals more than on family goals, and often on things more than on people. Most of us need to make two adjustments in our time management if it is to work for our families rather than against them. First, we need to adopt a serendipity attitude that allows us—even prompts us—to see unexpected, unplanned opportunities to do fun and beneficial things with our children. Second, we need to do all we can to block out certain times when we can be together as families.

It used to be that families ate dinner together most nights, and the dinner hour and the dinner table became the time and the place where things were discussed and feelings were shared. The busyness and conflicting schedules of today make that ideal virtually impossible for most families. But as a minimum, families with children living at home should set aside one or two regular, set times each week when they will be together for a meal. For many families, Sunday lunch or dinner is the best time for a family meeting setting. The next week's needs and schedule can be reviewed, parents can ask about anything from grades to friends, and kids can ask about anything from rules to finances. Family mission statements can be developed. It's a time to share feelings and to feel the teamwork and identity of family.

In addition to the weekly family meeting (on Sunday or whenever), families ought to try to set one weekday evening aside as a family night where they do something fun together—something as simple as a movie or a visit to the pizza house or the ice cream store. It may not be possible to do this every week (or to hold the family meeting every Sunday), but if times are set aside and if only real emergencies or things beyond our control cancel them, they will begin to have a bonding, unifying effect on our families. Whether a family consists of two people or ten, setting aside certain times of the week for just being together can make a huge difference.

We had been having Sunday family meetings for years, as consistently as our schedules would allow. But we still didn't feel as though everyone was hav-

ing their say or that all were equally involved. Then we heard an idea from another family and began trying it in ours: Once a month, on the first Sunday of each month, after a Sunday lunch together, we began holding what we called a "family testimony meeting." Each family member had a chance to stand up for a few moments and talk about (or "testify" on) his or her feelings (about other members of the family, about school or work, about themselves)—their beliefs, their worries, their joys, etc. Each could just say whatever he or she wanted, with everyone else listening and paying attention. The only instruction we gave was that what we each said should center on feelings and use the words "I feel" as often as possible.

The first couple of times were a little slow—one child was too anxious to express himself, another didn't want to say a word. But we persevered, Linda and I talking about our feelings (especially for the children) and then encouraging them to do the same. It has now become the absolute highlight of our month. There, in the quiet of our living room, with phones off the hook, we take time to tell each other how we feel. The love level and the trust level have expanded dramatically. The "first Sunday testimonies" have helped us know each other better, appreciate each other more, and love each other more completely.

Find your own formula. Look for the times of the week that are most possible and most predictable for you. Then prioritize them and make them happen. Real quality time will come gradually, and according to your willingness to set time aside and to be flexible and spontaneous when relationship opportunities come up.

Remember that this third essential element is all about reinventing time management. There are three alterations or additions you can make in whatever planner or time-management system you use. These three adjustments are guaranteed to focus your priorities more on your family.

1. The "Serendipity Line"

On your daily planner page or your "to-do" list, draw a top-to-bottom line down the middle of the page. Write down your schedule, your plans, and your list exactly as you usually do, but write it on the left-hand side of your page. Leave the right side blank, but write at the top "Serendipities."

Spontaneity and serendipity are important for parents because when a teaching moment or an opportunity to really communicate with a child comes up, it usually is not planned, and if we're not flexible enough to adjust our schedule a bit, we miss the opportunity.

Serendipity is defined as "a state of mind in which, through awareness and sagacity, a person frequently finds something good while seeking something else." Challenge yourself to have at least three "serendipities" every day. Be willing to jump across the serendipity line—from structure and plans to flexibility and opportunity—especially when it involves a need or an opportunity with your spouse or one of your children. It could be something as simple as planning to answer a child's question rather than rushing out the door, or taking a moment together to look at a newly opened flower. At the end of each day, write down your "serendipities" on the right-hand side of your page. Learn to value them and to watch for them.

2. The "Priority Blanks"

At the top of that same daily planning page or to-do list, make three short horizontal lines and, as you plan (before listing your schedule and your have-to-dos), take a moment and write down three "choose-to-dos"—one for your family, one for yourself, and one for your work. By definition, a choose-to-do is not a necessity or a requirement like "attend the meeting" or "make the call" or "pick up the kids after soccer." Come up with your three "choose-to-dos" by thinking about needs. "What is one little thing that my child really needs from me today?" "What is one thing that I need today—some small thing I can do for myself?" "What is a need at work that doesn't have to be addressed but that I'd like to do?" By thinking about and writing down three choose-to-dos *before* you begin to list the have-to-dos, you become more balanced. The three key priorities or stewardships for your life (family, work, and self) get addressed and get some attention every day, and no matter how hectic and beyond your control the rest of the day gets, you have controlled and decided on the things that matter most. The cumulative impact of these daily choose-to-dos (seven little things each week for family, for self, thirty per month, 365 per year) can be powerful!

3. The "Relationship Bands"

The third and final adjustment is the simplest of all. Just make three horizontal bands across your daily planning page—perhaps with a highlighting pen—one early in the morning, one as you return home from work in the evening, and one late at night. Don't plan anything in these bands. Reserve them for relationships and for just being there for your family—at breakfast, at dinner, and at bedtime. Just drop out of your plans and schedule and *be there* with your spouse and children for whatever they need.

By applying these ideas and other, similar ones that you may come up with, you can begin to change how you think about planning and time management. You can reinvent the whole process so that it works *for* family commitment and family time instead of against them.

Learn to think of your job and your work as something you do to support your family rather than the other way around. Balance your life and your thinking by working as hard on family goals and plans as you do on career goals and plans. Remind yourself that inner relationships last longer and have more ultimate value than outer achievements.

As you do, you will become the owner of the third essential element!

Essential Element Four: Absolutely Insist on and Be Committed to COMMUNICATION

Far too many marriages and parent-child relationships suffer in silence. Feelings go unexpressed. Resentments or misunderstandings grow because they are unresolved. Pride makes people walk away rather than come together or compromise or apologize. Kids rebel and leave home or go silent because they're convinced that parents don't (and can't) understand them. When parents try to show interest or ask questions, it comes across as interrogation. Couples find themselves doing more judging and demanding than real sharing and supporting and communicating. Within our families, where the deepest intimacy should exist, we resort to small talk on safe subjects and avoid the real issues, the real needs, the real worries. And it's all exacerbated in today's high-tech world, where more and more kids find communication with computers easier and less threatening than communication with people. They learn more from movies and TV and the Internet than from parents, because they spend vastly more time there, and see and hear far more words from the screen than they hear from their parents' mouths.

One problem, of course, is that communication takes time. And in this busy world of overcommitment and trying to do everything, it is the time for needed relationships that is so often lost. We trade relationships for achievements. We trade communication for busyness. We trade time spent talking for time spent running around and trying to keep up with all those we view as competitors. These are always bad trade-offs, but we get in the habit of doing them.

The old stalwarts (and symbols) of communication—family dinners, long walks, bedtime stories, Sunday drives—just don't happen much anymore, replaced in families by TV and ball games and electronics and more meetings and lessons than our parents could have imagined.

But it's not just the places and traditions of communication that are gone, it's the desire and the effort.

How do we restore it all—the desire, the effort, and the traditions? We start with the realization that everything that matters most—our happiness, our values, and our families—depends on communication. Then, having lifted communication to the status of highest priority, we devote ourselves to us. We put nothing ahead of it, we insist on it, we demand it of ourselves and ask and work and plead for it from those we love. We develop traditions of communication in our families and we take steps to break the patterns of noncommunication that may have developed.

In terms of specific approaches, here are some starters for each:

Creating communication traditions in the family. Develop some regular rituals, repetitive things that you do "in family" that stimulate communication. Examples of some that have worked in other families:

- Bedtime "happy's or sad's." As you tuck a child in bed ask, "What was your 'happy' today? Your 'sad'?" Over the course of many evenings, you'll learn a lot about your child's friends, social situations, school, fears, etc.

- Active listening. After you ask, listen actively by paraphrasing back to your child each thing he or she says to you. This shows interest and nonjudgment. Instead of interrogating or directing or drawing conclusions, just rephrase whatever your child says. "So you felt bad when Lisa sat with someone else at lunch." When you listen without directing, kids will jump from subject to subject—often from effect to cause—and will tell you things you'd never think to ask! Practice the same technique with your spouse.

As a young father I [] had an experience that combined the goal-setting and active-listening methods of communication.

I read about active listening, or Rogerian technique (named after famous therapist Carl Rogers), and will never forget the first time I consciously tried it. Seven-year-old Saydi, rather caught up with her friends and not always easy to talk to, had written for her weekly school goal, "Get a new friend." The normal parental response would have been either a challenge, "Why, don't you have enough friends?" or a lecture, "You know, to have friends you have to be a friend," but I was trying the Rogerian technique so I simply said, "I see, you want to find a new friend this week at school." "Yes," said Saydi, "because my best friend Katie was so rude to me."

Again I avoided the typical parental response, "What did she do?" or "Do I need to call her mom?" I just said, "Oh, I see. The reason your goal is a new friend is that Katie hasn't been so nice to you." Magically, Saydi went right on, telling me everything, really communicating. "Yes. See, she was the chooser in soccer and she didn't even pick me for her team." I just kept paraphrasing back what she said, and ten minutes later I knew more about her second-grade life and about her feelings than I could have learned through hours of interrogation-type questioning.

• Goals and "consulting." Even fairly small children can set goals for the week. On Sunday, ask a child to set three goals for the week ahead: one for school (for example, a high test score, a paper turned in); one for personal development (sports, music, scouting); and one for family (cleaning a room, fixing something, sweeping the walk). Set the example by setting your own weekly goal for each of the same three categories (substituting work for school). Then explain your goals to one another. It will lead to a lot of communication about a lot of subjects, and you will feel (to yourself and to your child) more like a consultant helping with his goals and less like a pushy manager trying to get kids to follow your goals and agenda.

- Sunday dinners. While the old family-dinner concept may have pretty well lost out to fast food and overcommitted schedules, once a week is still realistic. Pick a day and reserve dinner. Use the time to talk about schedules for the week and then ask one another questions about feelings, dreams, priorities, and concerns. (This may become the weekly family meeting discussed earlier.)

- Car time. All that time we spend driving kids to school, to lessons, and so forth—time we usually resent—can be "captive" communication time. Ask "interest questions" ("I'm interested in that new math teacher. How is she?") rather than "interrogation questions" ("How's your grade in math?").

- "Dates." Married couples who still have a weekly or biweekly date on a set night tend to keep a courtship mentality that prompts better communication and a more lasting romance. A variation on the theme works for kids—a "daddy date" or "mommy date" for which the child decides what to do and where to go.

- "1 to 10." When kids have a hard time talking about their feelings—or where you're getting just "yes" or "no" or "fine" answers to your questions—try the "ranking" technique. Say, "I'm going to mention five separate things to you and you rank how worried you are about them from 1 to 10." "Ranking" works on everything from how much they enjoyed a date to how important they perceive various things to be. Once they've ranked something, it gets easier to talk about and to ask further "active listening" questions about whatever the subject is.

- "Interviews." This approach will fail or be counterproductive if you approach it like an interrogation or a checklist. If your questions sound like a judgmental evaluation, you'll get short, defensive answers. If you ask, "How are your grades?" or "How are you doing with your friends?," you'll get one-word answers like "Fine" and "Okay" and your child's goal will be to "get this over with." Instead, start off with things like, "Son, I love you so much and I'm so proud of you. I just want to know as much as I can about what's happening in your life and what you're thinking. Tell me what's going on in school lately." Then practice active listening. You decide on the frequency of your interviews, but when they are regular, they work best (for example, every Sunday afternoon, or the second Sunday of each month).

Breaking patterns of noncommunication. When you're not talking—when the trust level and communication level have dipped pretty much to the nonexistent level with a child—some more drastic jump-start techniques are in order.

- A long trip. Take a child one-on-one on a long trip (preferably a long car trip). It could be a business trip (it may be expensive and inconvenient, but it can pay huge dividends) or a long weekend trip, or a hike or camp-out, or anything else you can conjure up. Just being alone together while traveling allows communication to develop. Don't push too hard, and don't interrogate. Use the techniques of active listening, ranking, and interest questions. Be willing to talk about things you're not particularly interested in. Let it develop. Express your joy in being together. Express your confidence and love and tell the child he is your priority and you are committed to him unconditionally. Be satisfied with small progress. Don't expect one trip to solve everything.

- Letters or e-mail. Some kids communicate better in writing, even if they live in the same house with you. E-mail them, write them notes. Let your written communication open up opportunities for verbal communication. Some children talk more openly on the phone than they do face to face. Have some unpressured phone conversations to open up the channels and to get things "warmed up" for one-on-one time spent together.

- Surrogates. Sometimes kids will talk better and say more to anyone else but you. If there's an uncle or aunt or a friend—or anyone you trust who can spend some time one-on-one with a noncommunicative child and get him talking—it can furnish you with needed information and can open up future possibilities for your own communication.

- Discussion of communication "proverbs." Discuss the adage "Some things are better left unsaid." Is it true? Is it true within families? Should we hide anything from one another or have secrets? (There may be bad timing and bad ways to say things, but families should look for chances to share everything.) Discuss a second saying, "Unexpressed feelings never die, they just come forth later in uglier forms." Is that one true? How important is it to talk about our feelings?

- Persist! Whichever of these ideas (or others) you try, tell your child that communication with him or her means everything to you and that you'll work on it forever. Keep trying, look for opportunities, make time together. Do whatever it takes to open up the channels.

The reason we list each of these individual ideas is that as we write, we're thinking of times we've had to call on these methods to save communication with our own kids. How well we remember our e-mails with Josh, our long drives with Noah, phone calls with Saydi. Notes back and forth with Charity. Goal discussions with Talmadge. Different things work at different times with different kids—and something will work sometime with every child.

The simple fact is that we give up too easily on communication. We expect too little from it. When it gets hard, we back off and do something easier and more pleasant. When a kid (or a spouse) says, "I can't talk to you," we either get mad ("I can't talk to you either") or sad ("I guess that's just the way it is"), rather than getting determined and saying, at least to ourselves, "We've got to find a way!"

Everything depends on communication. It's what solves problems; it's what draws people together; it's how love grows; it's what builds trust and security and identity. It is too important ever to give up on. Simply make up your mind that communication is going to happen in your family. Establish traditions that facilitate it; break the patterns that inhibit it. Be committed to communication, and in that commitment you will find the fourth essential element!

Summary of Solution One (the First Four Elements)

As we parents think about the first problem of overbusy lifestyles and hearts that are turned to the wrong priorities, we all must remember one very basic thing: We are not talking about other people here, or about society at large. These are our own individual lifestyles and our own personal hearts and our own unique and particular families and we do have control over them.

We control them by a simple two-step process: (1) recognizing and understanding what has gone wrong and what forces are working against us, and (2) doing the things that restore the essential elements of family.

Our lifestyles and priorities can be completely renewed and our families reoriented as we take the steps to restore (1) recommitment, (2) purpose, (3) family time management, and (4) communication.

Sometimes just resolving to change is the biggest part of the battle—saying, in essence, "This is my family and my home. I'm not going to let the world and the larger society dictate how it works or thinks. We'll manage our own lives and set our own patterns of commitment, communication, and purpose."

We live in a fast current of swirling change, information, and dangerous turbulence, but by establishing the first four elements, parents can make their homes islands that withstand and yet benefit from the current rather than floating logs that are swept along, sucked up, and eventually broken apart.

Create a Solid,

Lasting Family Institution

That Preempts and Supersedes

Other Institutions

As individual concerned parents who have become aware of the dangers of large, relatively new institutions that are destructive to families, we have three options open to us: (1) give up and give in to entities and influences that are so much bigger than we are; (2) try to organize and fight against the "enemies" (anything from boycotts to letters to our congressmen); (3) create a family institution strong enough to resist the dangers posed by the larger institutions and false paradigms.

This section is for parents who choose the third option. Not that there is anything wrong with option two—in fact, some ideas along its lines make up the closing chapter of this book. But most of us, as parents, know that the thing we have the best chance of influencing, in the short term, is our own families. And we know, deep down, that if we put forth the effort, seek the right help, and stick with it, we can be the predominant influence in our own families and with our own children, countering, pre-empting, and superseding the negative influences of larger institutions and false paradigms.

> I [Linda] remember one of my first personal experiences with the alternating helplessness and hopefulness that all parents feel. Our oldest was twelve and completely caught up with her peer group. She seemed to have total interest in her friends and zero interest in her family. And I knew at least a couple of her friends were not providing the kind of influence we'd have wished for. Any time she had apart from her friends she wanted to spend in front of the TV or listening to music, both of which were blasting her with the wrong values and attitudes. "Where's my influence?" I thought. "How can I have any effect on who she's becoming?"
>
> Then, at a parent-teacher conference, I saw an essay she'd written. The assignment (and the title) was "My Hero," and she had written about me. I realized that the opportunity for influence and for the relationship I wanted with her were there—would always be there—but I had to make it happen.

The bottom line is that we must *turn our hearts* to our children and our families. We must come to understand that the larger institutions that were created to serve us are now demanding too much service from us—and too much time and too much allegiance. We must, as parents, make a conscious decision to give those institutions less of our time, and to give them none of our hearts. Our personal trade-offs must favor the family. As we turn our hearts, we will also turn our minds, our priorities, and our time.

Every organization or entity that lasts and endures (from a school to a fraternity to a company) has five things that allow it to survive and to thrive (and that give its members the identity, security, and motivation that hold them): (1) rules/boundaries/order (laws and patterns of behavior that protect other members and preserve the whole); (2) an economy (a way of dividing work and having all members contribute to the bottom line); (3) traditions (which provide enjoyment as well as identity, unity, and permanence); (4) a heritage and a history (to be proud of and to identify with); and (5) an understanding of where it fits in the broader scheme of things.

The large institutions that are both the culprits and the benefactors with regard to families have all five of these. Parents must be sure that their own little family institutions also have all four, so they can be as permanent and as strong as the big institutions that they must both use and protect themselves from.

These five (rules, economy, traditions, history, and understanding) are the fifth, sixth, seventh, eighth, and ninth essential elements. Together, they create an infrastructure that makes a family work efficiently and that provides individual family members with the support and help (identity, security, and motivation) that they need to be happy, successful people. Like the infrastructure of a city (roads, bridges, water systems), a family infrastructure takes time and effort to build, but once it is in place, it saves time and makes everything more efficient.

Essential Element Five: A "Family Legal System" of RULES

With hindsight, we can see that our own first effort to set up family laws was rather comical. As young parents with our three young children, we tried to create a list of family rules by nomination (I think, back then, we still thought a family was a democracy!). The kids chimed in with everything from "Don't hit anyone" to "Never plug in plugs—you could get shocked." We dutifully listed every one on a big chart and we soon had thirty-seven "family laws." No one really remembered them or paid much attention to them, and one day our seven-year-old complained, "Dad, even in the Bible there's only ten rules!"

Over the years we figured it out. We needed a small number of very simple rules, each with a clear consequence for breaking it but with a provision for repentance by which apologetic children could avoid the consequence or penalty. It finally came down to five one-worders:

PEACE: Or you sit on the "repenting bench" with the other "fighter" until you can say what *you* did wrong—"it takes two to tangle"—and give the other kid a hug and ask him to forgive you.

RESPECT: Or we'll start over until you get it right and give a respectful answer. If I ask you to take out the garbage and you whine about it or give an excuse, I'll start over and try to ask you very politely but very directly, "Son, please take out the garbage." The emphasized "please" is a trigger word to remind the child that he needs to respond respectfully and that you'll keep starting over until he does.

ORDER: Get your room straight or face the penalty that you can't go anywhere until you clean it up.

ASKING: We want to always know where you are, so if you forget to ask, the next time you want to go somewhere the answer will be no. The same penalty applies to curfew.

OBEDIENCE: You can ask why and I'll try to tell you, and possibly even reconsider, but only ask why once and then obey. Remember, someday you'll be the parent.

Looking back now, over twenty-five years of trying to establish and live these five family laws, we find that some of our most cherished memories are wrapped up in them (from heated curfew discussions to everyone pitching in to help a child get his room cleaned up so he could go out without breaking a law).

Some of our most interesting memories center around the law of PEACE and the "repenting bench." Somehow we ended up with incredibly strong-willed children, and "sibling rivalries" is a pretty mild term for describing the competing, arguing, and outright fighting that crop up so predictably. We came to the "repenting bench" idea because there was no way that we, as parents, could resolve everything. Trying to figure out who was right and who was wrong—being the judge and jury, trying to decide who to punish and how—was exhausting. And we wanted (needed) the kids to learn how to resolve things for themselves.

Our "repenting bench" is a short, uncomfortable pew that we got out of an old church. The rule is simple: Any two family members who are fighting (arguing, yelling, disagreeing) have to sit together on that bench until each can tell what he did wrong (not what the other person did) and can, with a hug, say to the other, "I'm sorry. Will you forgive me?" We stressed that both of the "fighters" are always partly to blame.

Oh, the "repenting" we've seen! From kids who had to sit there for half an hour trying to figure out what they did wrong, to kids who repent on their way to the bench so they won't have to sit there at all. The hugs and the "sorrys," even if their main motivation is to escape the bench, have blunted bad feelings a thousand times and contributed to our children's love for one another and to their capacity to work out their own conflicts.

Each of the four other laws has an equally interesting history and has become a part of the fabric of our family.

Family laws need regular discussion and recommitment. Setting them up in the first place needs to be a highly communicative process. Kids need to understand that the purposes of laws are safety and happiness and that they show an increase, not a decrease, of trust and of love.

Laws and rules—lovingly set, explained, and implemented—provide children with security and with a clear manifestation of a parent's love and concern. Emphasize repeatedly that laws are about safety and happiness in living together. Compare them to traffic laws, to civic laws, to school rules. *Tell* them that laws show our love and concern for one another and show our desire to have a good, orderly family in which the family members care for one another—a family that gets us ready for life on our own.

Tell children that the reason you have so *few* laws is that you trust them and know they will always try to make good decisions. Explain that a few good rules can keep a family safe and strong and give its members more freedom. A lesson can be learned by the way three separate kennels raised puppies:

The first kennel has a very small yard and a very large number of rules and procedures. Only one puppy at a time was let out of his cage to eat. The only exercise was to run back and forth in a tightly fenced dog run. The puppies could do only what their keepers allowed them to do at any given moment and they were always closely supervised.

The second kennel was just the opposite. There were no fences and no schedule and no rules. The pups could go and do whatever they wanted. The attendant just threw out some food once or twice a day for them to fight over.

The third kennel had a big yard, where the puppies had lots of options and made lots of decisions. But there was a high fence around the edge that kept them safe and each puppy had his own feeding bowl.

The "high fence" is some simple, solid, well-explained, and clearly defined family rules that carry predictable penalties for breaking. The big yard is trusting parents who give children lots of leeway and room for decisions *within* the fence.

Your own laws and rules in your own family may be different from ours, but the principles behind them should be the same: simplicity, consistency, "natural consequence" penalties, and a provision for "repentance" to avoid the penalty.

As children get older, other rules (like curfews) can be added. The rules should always be discussed, understood, and agreed upon and you should constantly emphasize that the rules are about safety and about concern for each other, not about a lack of trust or confidence in each other.

As your own family laws are developed and refined, you will be giving yourself and your family a great gift, and you will become the possessors of the fifth essential element!

Essential Element Six: A "Family ECONOMY"

I [Richard] remember the exact day that I started worrying about the effects of allowances. I was lying in bed on a Saturday morning when our three small children (five, seven, and nine) burst into our bedroom with their hands out, shouting, "We want our money." Something about it was too much like a welfare line. They were demanding the money that their allowance entitled them to, and there was no connection in their minds either to anything they'd had to do to earn the money or to any responsibility for what they did with it or how they spent it.

What lessons was this teaching them? All the wrong ones, it seemed.

Linda and I had a short trip scheduled that weekend and we used the travel time to work on a new system. Some friends had told us about a "star chart" system they'd devised, and we designed a "peg system" along the same lines. Each child would have a simple pegboard with four pegs. They could put in the first one when they got up and to breakfast on their own and were ready for school on time. They could put in the second peg when they had checked and tidied up their "zone," their part of the house or yard, and the third peg when their homework and music practice were done. The fourth peg went in if and when they had their teeth brushed and their pajamas on by their bedtime. Each peg would translate into a point on the slip they could put into the family bank for that day. Saturdays would become "payday" rather than "welfare-line day," and they could choose to save some of their "earned" money in a family bank that would pay interest. The total they could earn each week would be significantly more than their previous allowances, so that they could start buying their own clothes and personal effects.

Just as they are made more secure by rules and limits, kids are made more confident and competent by responsibility. A strong family institution needs a way to teach responsibility and to divide and share the work of the household and a way of letting kids earn a small share in the family's income. Here is one way to do so. (Each family should tailor-make its own. This approach works best for kids between six and twelve. If you can start it during those years, it can work into the teens.)

Caution: Don't try to set this up overnight. It will take a lot of discussion and some trial and error. Remember that infrastructures take time to build, but then they save time.

1. *Do a big chart of all the household work that exists. List everything, from doing the breakfast dishes to sweeping the patio. Explain that those who do a share of the work should get a share of the money that comes into a family. While everyone should take care of his or her own room without pay, there are plenty of "common areas" in the house and yard that need to be taken care of and daily tasks that someone needs to do, and those who do them should share in the family income.*

2. *Tell kids that this approach will allow them to earn more than they could get as an allowance and that with their earnings they can buy*

their own clothes. Kids in this elementary-school age range are flattered by responsibility. (Note that this system doesn't require any additional money. Parents are simply taking the funds they spend on children's clothes and channeling that money through the kids, who earn it and make their own purchase decisions—learning economic and motivational lessons through the whole process.)

3. *Explain that there are four things each person can get "credit" for each day: (a) getting up and being ready for school on time; (b) one "zone" or area of the house or yard (not their own room) that they make sure is clean and in order; (c) homework (and music practice if applicable) for each evening; and (d) being ready for and in bed by bedtime. Each day they can fill in a slip (on their own initiative, without a lot of reminding from you) with a 1, 2, 3, or 4, depending on how many of the four they did. You "initial" the completed slip to make it official.*

4. *The slips go in a box, or "family bank," and Saturday becomes payday, when a child receives an amount proportionate to the total of his slips. He can take his money in cash or leave it in the family bank. He is given a checkbook (an old or extra book of your checks) with which he can deposit money in the family bank (with a deposit slip) or draw it out (with a check). When he goes shopping with you, he brings his checkbook and writes a check out to you so you, in turn, can pay for what he buys. He keeps track of his balance in his check register.*

This "family economy" can be enhanced in a number of ways. A child can have an interest-paying savings account as well as a checking account in the family bank. Parents may want to pay a high interest rate on the condition that the savings be used only for college. When a child turns sixteen, real checking and savings accounts are opened for him at a local bank or a discount brokerage and all the money in his family bank account is transferred in. Children might also be encouraged to donate a certain percentage of what they earn to church or charity.

This type of family economy has been a huge blessing in our family. Kids have learned principles that will serve them well for the rest of their lives.

. . . About self-reliance: We recall nine-year-old Jonah calculating how much he'd have by age sixteen at the 10-percent-per-quarter interest we paid

on his "education only" family bank savings account. I also recall the look of pride on his eighteen-year-old face as he wrote out a real check for his full freshman year tuition.

. . . About the dangers of instant gratification: Eight-year-old Saydi spending $80 of "her own" money on a pair of designer jeans and wanting to "turn them back in" or sell them to someone the next week because she realized she had no money left in her checking account for other things that she wanted.

. . . About depreciation: Josh wanting to "sell-me-down" rather than hand-me-down the outgrown clothes he'd bought to his little brother, who wanted "a good deal."

. . . About restraint: Ten-year-old Talmadge saying he'd decided to ask himself three questions before he bought anything: "Do I want it," "Do I need it?," "Can I afford it?"

. . . About saving: Twelve-year-old Shawni observing, "When I put some money in savings right when I get it, it's like I never had it, so I don't miss it."

Good as the "money lessons" are, it's the life lessons that really count—lessons about responsibility, about delayed gratification, about self-reliance, and about doing your share.

Once again, this type of a responsibility-transferring family economy is a balanced middle ground between two much more common (and much less effective) practices in families. On one extreme, parents simply hand out money to kids—or buy things for them—on an as-needed basis. The child is completely void of responsibility. He asks his mom or dad for money whenever he needs (or wants) it, and whether he gets anything is more a product of a parent's mood than of the legitimacy of his request.

Over the years, this family economy has developed and grown and been adopted and modified by thousands of families. Kids make their own purchase decisions, save for college, figure out ways to motivate and remind themselves to fill out their slips, and assume a real part of the household workload. Some families have gone on to set up legally recognized family partnerships or limited-liability companies that can lend older children interest-free money for college tuition or to make down payments on their homes.

As with each of the eleven essential elements, a family economy is no "quick fix" and doesn't develop overnight. But also like each of the other elements, it is based on sound principles and it prepares kids to function in the real world.

It requires some constraint by parents, such as allowing a child to suffer the consequences of an inadequate wardrobe if he just hasn't earned the money to buy what he needs (we've been known to give a lot of underwear and socks as birthday presents), and it requires a long-term perspective, such as understanding that it's better for kids to learn from their money mistakes (paying too much for something, failing to save or budget) now while the amounts and consequences are small, rather than later (when they're away at college using your credit card).

This sixth element, like the others, will draw your family closer together, give you additional constructive things to communicate about, and become part of a lasting foundation for your children. While it uses money as the motivator and the median, it is less about money than it is about principles of responsibility and delayed gratification. A family economy can be a microcosm of the real world and can prepare children to cope with what is "out there." More important, it can teach the lessons that will help a child become a secure and happy adult.

Essential Element Seven: Family TRADITIONS

Everyone, particularly every child, needs an identity larger than himself—something he or she belongs to, feels part of, and gains security and protection from. It is kids who do not get this identity from their families who are drawn to the rituals, "colors," and traditions of gangs or other identity substitutes for families.

Strong traditions exist in every lasting institution—in schools, in fraternities, and certainly in families. Traditions are the glue that holds families together. Kids love and cling to family traditions because they are predictable and stable in an unpredictable world.

Almost all families have traditions, at least subconscious ones, often centering on holidays or other special occasions. But some parents come to realize the importance of traditions and the ability of good traditions to teach values to improve communication, to give security to kids, and to hold families together. Such parents can refine and redefine their family traditions and give them true and lasting bonding power.

Start by assessing and analyzing your own family traditions. What do you do on each holiday? Each family birthday? Do you have some weekly traditions, such as a special Sunday dinner? Are there some monthly traditions, such as going over the calendar and the family's schedule for the month ahead? Make a list of your yearly, monthly, and weekly traditions.

Then, as a family, ask yourself three questions: How much joy or how much fun comes from each tradition? What values are taught by each tradition? Are there some gaps—some months without a holiday or birthday tradition? With these questions in mind, revise and redesign your family traditions. Formalize them a little by writing them up on a chart or in a special book.

Here's a sampling of what happened to us as we went through this reassessing process:

1. *We revised some traditions. For example, our Thanksgiving tradition had essentially been to eat way too much and watch football all day on TV. We decided to shift the emphasis to thanks by making a collective list, on a long roll of cash register tape, of all the little things we are thankful for. Each year we try to "break the record" for the number of things listed.*

2. *We decided it would be good to have at least one major family tradition each month, to look forward to and anticipate. Most of these centered on a birthday or holiday, but there was nothing in May or September so we started a "welcome-spring day" (a hike) and a "welcome-fall day" (a picnic).*

3. *We listed all the traditions, by month, in a big, leather-bound book. A little description of each tradition appears on the left and a child's illustration of that activity appears on the right.*

Besides the once-a-year-type birthday or holiday traditions, there can be shorter-range traditions. Many families have religious traditions on Saturday or Sunday. There can be traditional ways of cooking a particular meal or of getting ready for school or of packing for a trip. Some traditions are real rituals, involving a particular sequence of events. There is comfort and security and identity in family rituals.

> *One other personal incident will illustrate the "staying power" and bonding influence of family traditions. On my [Richard's] birthday in October, we had always raked huge piles of leaves with the kids and then jumped in them, stuffed them in our shirts, thrown them in the air, and just generally had a wild time. We thought as the kids got older, their interest in such a frivolous activity would fade. On the contrary, when they were teens, the leaf piles just got bigger. Finally, one year, four of our children were away at school or living abroad. On my birthday, four birthday cards arrived. As I opened the first, a leaf fell out and a note, "Dad, I honored your birthday tradition. Here's a leaf from my jumping pile. I love you." Through my tears I opened the other three—and a leaf fell from each.*

The crazier you can make your traditions, the more they will be remembered. On Saydi's birthday, on August 12, we are usually at our summer home by a lake in the mountains of Idaho. We decided when she was just a tiny tot to have fun on her birthday by floating her cake. Each year we found something wild and weird to float her cake on. After the first few years, the neighbors watched for us to come down to the beach with the cake on this year's floatie and help us watch it as it drifted out into the waves to see if it floated or sank. They also loved eating it afterward, even if it was a little soggy. Since those early years, we have floated her cake in a "wild wave" public swimming pool, on a moat around a castle in England on a funny old life preserver while bystanders wondered if we were all crazy, and in the bathtub one year when we weren't near water. It is always crazy, always the glue that makes each parent and every sibling think of Saydi on August 12 and maybe even float a little cupcake in their own sink on her behalf. A little added surprise: Our second grandchild was born on Saydi's birthday. It was easy to figure out what her birthday tradition would be! Truly, family traditions are not only the glue that holds your immediate family together, they also help spread the joy of family love and memories down to the next generation!

Our first daughter, Saren, wrote of her feelings about family traditions in an earlier book.[23] She was twenty-three when she wrote:

I love traditions. Anyone in my family can confirm this fact. I've become a tradition traditionalist! All my life I've thrown tantrums over traditions that are dropped or changed or altered in any way. And I've always rejoiced in holidays that are just so, that include all the things I love, all the memories remade and relieved every year. I guess one reason I've always been so very attached to traditions is that they give security and create memories. Perhaps the two things that make a family the strongest are security and memories. I could go on forever on this subject, but here are a few favorite traditions.

At Christmas I've always delighted in assigning roles and dressing everyone up as members of Mary's family for our annual Nazareth Supper. That was always my job Christmas Eve night. How I loved sitting around the candlelit table, all of us swathed in sheets and wearing odd bits of cloth on our heads, talking together as if we were Bible characters and laughing as Dad tried to be so serious and Joseph started teasing Mary and the little kids picked weird names for themselves, like Llama and Hiawatha, and the kids all complained that they couldn't see their food and that they hated dates and figs—and "Where's the catsup for the fish?" "Jesus didn't eat catsup." "Really?" Those candlelit scenes will never, ever be erased from my memory.

I love Christmas mornings, when Josh always wakes up first—at about 3:30 or 4:00 A.M.—and wakes everyone else up. We all eagerly look in our stockings that Santa leaves on our bedposts and dump out all our candy and treats on the floor in Jonah's room so we can trade toys and candy and feast on oranges and candy canes until we're totally sick—and it's still only 4:30 A.M. Then we all excitedly sit on the stairs singing Christmas carols until Mom and Dad wake up and appear with messy hair and pj's and groggily make us line up to go into the living room—youngest to oldest, or shortest to tallest (I like that way, because then I'm nearly at the beginning). Dad goes in and turns on the Christmas tree lights and some Christmas music and finally all the kids rush into the room and search out presents from Santa with their name on them. We try to be organized—one present at a time—but in the end there's a mad rush of crumpled wrapping paper and kids running around with dolls and remote-control cars. Everything's opened before 6:00. Then we have a wonderful Christmas brunch of eggs benedict, where there's never quite enough hollandaise sauce or asparagus and we see our cousins and play our new board games and we fall asleep and we are so together. I could go on forever, but suffice it to say: I LOVE CHRISTMAS! And the traditions we have make every member of the family so vital, every moment so dear, every memory so perfect!

I also love birthday traditions. Some birthday traditions really stuck. Others didn't—and that's okay. On Dad's birthday, we always go to a park and rake up huge piles of leaves and jump in them and bury each other in them. For all my life, I'll always remember the time we were celebrating Dad's birthday in the leaves and Mom and Dad announced another baby would be joining the family. What joy that was! And I remember one birthday Dad had when we went to the park in the pouring rain and sat together in the van—looking at the wet leaves and remembering together so much we'd shared. Autumn leaves will always remind me of Dad and joy. And I'll always be overcome by an urge to go jump in them!

You know what I really miss, now that I'm over here in Bulgaria? I miss the simple things—like coming home from something and just sitting in the kitchen talking to Mom about my day, or taking Charity to the store with me to buy something or hanging out with Saydi, talking about boys and school and friends all night on my big bed. I miss helping Jonah wallpaper his room and having him come put his arm around me. I miss Dad sitting at the kitchen table late at night, telling me to come sit down by him and talk awhile as I walk through. I miss talking to Eli as he sits on the repenting bench about what he needs to tell Dad and Mom so he can get off the bench (he'll be mad at me for writing that). I miss talking to Noah about his girl-friends or having him come give me a hug—just because. I miss Talmadge sticking his head out the door to the garage as I back out in the car, yelling, "Be sure to wear your seat belt!" I miss Shawni coming into my room, early in the morning while I'm still asleep, and asking which shoes look best with her outfit. I miss Josh's gentle smile and I miss him showing me cool things I never would have noticed on my own. I miss long drives home from Jackson Hole or Bear Lake, singing all the family songs or complaining because Dad wants us to sing the family songs or because we're crowded or hungry. I miss laughter together. I miss making cookies with the little kids and eating all the dough before we can get around to baking it. I miss a million other little everyday things.

All these little things come from the trust and love we feel for each other. And I really believe that all this trust and love come from the patterns and traditions that Mom and Dad helped us set, the examples they showed us, and the little things we did every day.

In that same book, we spoke of eight "basic strengths" to look for, to design into your family traditions:

Today many good recipe books include what each serving will give you in terms of calories, fat grams, vitamins, and so forth. As we decide what traditions we want to continue cooking and serving up in our families, we need to pay attention to what's in them and what we get out of them.

The first criterion for a good tradition is simply that it brings family members together, strengthening the ties that bind us to one another and making joyful memories. Every tradition that does this is worth keeping regardless of whether it does anything else. In fact, another definition of a good tradition is "a practice or habit that unites family members and enhances their joy."

There are at least eight other aspects of life that family traditions can help us to understand and develop. Let's look at them together and then define them one at a time.

- VALUES: All good traditions, by definition, promote certain values, such as loyalty and unity. Certain traditions directly promote a particular value—for example, many Christian traditions reinforce generosity.

- COMMUNICATION: Many traditions can improve communication between family members.

- EDUCATION: Some traditions can improve your children's education—by reinforcing ideas or concepts they are learning in school or in many cases introducing history, values, or ways of thinking that schools leave out.

- MARRIAGE: Some traditions, when practiced in two-parent families, can strengthen the marriage relationship and partnership.

- RESPONSIBILITY: Some traditions help improve children's (and adults') abilities to accept responsibility, to set goals, and to be independent and self-reliant.

- SENSITIVITY: Some traditions increase family members' tolerance, empathy, and respect for others.

- INDIVIDUALITY: Some traditions increase children's sense of individual confidence and uniqueness, help with their sense of identity, and offer parents opportunities to praise their children's individual gifts and unique talents.

- GUIDANCE: Some very special traditions have a certain "light" or "magic" about them and may invoke a spiritual connection, guidance, or direction from a higher power.

Take some time and review your family traditions. Do they help you in teaching values and in developing better communication? Adjust and alter to make your traditions productive as swell as enjoyable. List them by month in a special book of some kind or put them on a family calendar so they can be anticipated and planned for. Make them a priority until they take on a life of their own.

Essential Element Eight:
Family Genealogy, Family History, and ROOTS

Words like *history* and *genealogy* don't strike most of us as particularly exciting. Yet when we put the word *family* in front of them, they can become what may be the most powerful and effective approach of all for building strong and confident identity within our children.

Children with a sense of where they came from (and who they came from) have a kind of security and a kind of motivation that can't exist otherwise. Children are quick to grasp and understand that they descended from their parents, their grandparents, and their great-grandparents and that they inherited a big part of their physical, mental, and emotional selves from these ancestors. By teaching our children a little genetics and a little genealogy, we can help them understand why they have certain gifts, characteristics, interests, and abilities. A child who grows up feeling linkages, ties, security, and identity from and within an ongoing family will feel no need to seek these same things from a gang or an Internet chat room or some set of valueless persons portrayed on TV.

It's truly beautiful to see a child or adolescent who is proud of the shape of his nose or his hair color or his stature because it's a lot like a grandparent's, or a child who feels she can do well in math because her great-grandfather was good with numbers, or who makes a decision to be honest because of a story about an ancestor who made a difficult honest choice. Adopted children or stepchildren can find the same kind of identity through the social or attitudinal characteristics a parent passes on from his parents or grandparents.

Kids possess an inherent sense that "blood is thicker than water" and that who they are really does come from their family. The trick for parents is to make genealogy and family history so interesting that kids gravitate to it joyfully and naturally.

FAMILY TREE AND ANCESTOR IDENTITY

One of the best things we ever did in our family was to create a big "family tree," with pictures of our children's parents (2), grandparents (4), great-grandparents (8), and great-great-grandparents (16). We actually painted a big old oak tree on a 2-by-4-foot framed canvas. The tree has nine branches, each with a picture of one of the children. Branches go out from each of these nine, suggesting the children they will someday have. Our own two pictures (Mom and Dad) are on the trunk. Four roots go down from the trunk, each with a photo of a grandparent, and each of these splits into two so there is a total of eight smaller roots, each with a picture of a great-grandparent. In our case we were lucky enough to find photos of the next generation back—sixteen great-great-grandparents, which are glued onto the next and lowest set of sixteen sub-roots.

Something about this tree painting with its quaint, old-fashioned pictures is remarkably reassuring to our children. They look at it more than you would imagine. I [Linda] will never forget our seven-year-old one day, idly tracing with his finger a path from his limb down through the trunk and into the roots. "I'm one-fourth like you," he said, pointing at one of his grandpas. "And I'm one-eighth like you" as his finger went down to one of his great-grandmothers.

You don't need a complete gallery of four generations to do this in your family. Just grandparents will do, and any great-grandparents that you may happen to have a picture of. Once you've got some old photos on a tree, decide on some method for building on "ancestor identity." We know one family that makes videotapes of living grandparents telling about their childhoods. Another takes short vacations to the places where their ancestors came from. Still another celebrates birthdays of dead ancestors, complete with a birthday cake and candles, remembering and passing on all they know about them. The main thing is to create positive connections and to help your children feel a security and a heritage that they are proud of, that they are motivated by, that they can identify with.

If you'd like some help in tracing your family tree back a few generations, assistance is readily available through various genealogy or family-history associations. One quick way to start a search is to go to www.familysearch.org on the Internet, where anyone can access the Mormon Church's worldwide archives, the largest and most extensive in the world. With a minimum of name and date and location information you can quickly access what data is available on each root of your family tree.

ANCESTOR STORIES

A cruise ship seems an odd place to learn one of life's most important lessons, but several years ago we were doing some parenting workshops on a cruise ship in the Caribbean. One of our workshops was called "Teaching Children Values." The audience was older than what we were used to—lots of grandparents in attendance, and after the lecture one little grandmother came up to us and said, "I liked what you had to say about teaching children honesty and courage and peaceableness, but you've got to make those things a part of who they are, and "you can't know who you are until you know where you came from! They need to know their ancestors!" Her comment struck a chord with us, because it was true and it motivated us on our "Ancestor Book."

Occasionally, through reading family histories we found stories that we felt were important for our children to know. Assured that the kids would not be likely to be interested in the story if we suggested that we were going to read from a family history book at dinner, we decided instead to turn the most interesting stories into children's stories. We rewrote the stories in the language of children, with a promise, when the children were young, that if they listened carefully to the story we had written in a special book, that they would be allowed to illustrate the story for their own children and grandchildren to see. Young children don't start believing that they aren't artists until someone at school tells them that or they have a bad experience in an art class, so the illustrations for the stories we composed were much more interesting than the stories themselves. Seeing their idea of what happened, be it via stick people or quite remarkable artwork, was so fun! To this day when I think of the story entitled "The Mountain Moving Family," I can see hundreds of little people crammed on a huge sailing ship that Shawni drew as she illustrated the story. The faces of our own ancestors in the picture ranged from the mother, who was sadly thinking about her oldest child, who had died just before their departure, to the wildly excited looks on the faces of the children, who were up for an adventure.

One of the kids' favorite stories from the ancestor book was called "Grampa Dan and the Cat Who Came Back." It was about our Great Grandpa Dan Swenson, who was living in Sweden with his family of nine brothers and sisters. His father was a poor schoolteacher who was doing his best to feed and provide for his family. Dan had a cat that he adored, but one day his father came to him and told him that their family could no longer afford to feed the cat. His father explained that he could barely afford to keep his own children alive and that there was just not enough food to sustain the cat as well.

Dan was heartsick, but understood his father's despair. Though he tried several ways to remove the cat from the family, including taking him to the countryside and letting him loose, hoping that someone would find him and be able to care for him, the cat somehow always managed to find his way home. Though it was very difficult for Dan's father, he at last told Dan that they were going to tie the cat in a gunny sack along with a heavy rock and throw it into the river, assuring Dan that drowning was surely a better death than starving. With a tearstained face, Dan lovingly tied the cat in the bag with a large rock and threw the bag into the river from a bridge near their home. Dan sobbed all the way home. As he and his father turned the last corner, they could hardly believe their eyes when they saw a gray mass sitting on their front doorstep. It was Dan's beloved cat, carefully preening and systematically licking the last of the water from his fur.

"Any cat that dedicated to my son deserves to live! Somehow we'll come up with a way to feed the poor thing," declared Dan's dad in disbelief. What *a great lesson this story has been for our children in knowing not only the poverty but the determination and love of their forefathers.*

Another fun story is called "Why We're Not Billionaires." It involves Great-Great-Grandfather Erastus Bingham, a Mormon pioneer, who was clearing and farming his new land, having just emigrated from England. One day his plow turned up a big chunk of copper ore that had been buried in the furrow. He took the ore sample to Brigham Young, who was the leader of the immigrants in the valley. After an inspection of the ore, Brigham said, "Erastus, you'll be a happier man if you bury that ore and continue plowing," which Erastus did without question. Today, on that sight stands the biggest open-pit copper mine in the world: the Bingham Copper Mine.

Though our younger kids didn't appreciate what Grandpa Bingham gave up in continuing to be a farmer rather than a miner, I'm sure the thought has crossed a few of our teenagers' minds that a new car might be easier to come by had we inherited the millions of dollars that would have followed Grandpa Bingham had he decided to mine the ore. But they agree that the lessons learned about wisdom and obedience that have come through that line of ancestry are more important.

Our ancestors' stories of determination, subordination, exhilaration, devotion, and even dejection have been a part of our children's lives as they have grown up. Interestingly, the stories have become even more important now that many of them are grown. Something about knowing that the blood of their grandmother Jacobson, who was a great athlete before it was totally acceptable for a woman to be an athlete, has meant something to them. When they remember that she drove a team of horses from the time that she was a ten-year-old as well as taught each of about a thousand kids in the school system that they were gifted and talented and another thousand how to play the piano, they know that their gene pool is charged with something special. When the going gets tough, they remember that grandma, at seventy-five, jumped so fast at a women's volleyball game, that her wig fell off. Remembering that she swooped it up, put it on the volleyball pole, and played the rest of the game without it says something to our daughters who are young mothers who never seem to have time to do their hair.

Stories of honesty and courage have given our children the determination to continue that family trait. One story of Richard's father is about the night he accidentally backed into another car just after he got his driver's license.

Mortified and terrified, he left, and after some deliberation, dared to tell his father, who took him back to the scene of the accident and then up and down the streets in their small town until they found the owner of the car to apologize and pay for the damages.

Our children are surrounded by "out-of-world experiences" provided by hours of playing video games, surreal computer games, and movies that eject them into worlds beyond those of our wildest dreams when we were children. How important it is for them to have the anchor of the now out-of-world experiences of their own ancestors. Though all the stories you discover may not be of valor and integrity, they will all be learning experiences. Every bit of information learned about the lives of their forefathers helps them to know not only who they are but also what they can become! When names on a genealogical chart are connected to real-life stories about someone who makes up their gene pool, those names become real-life people who can help them figure out who they really are and enable them to become better parents themselves.

Simple Genetics Lesson

Something else that may help your children feel more connected and more appreciative of their extended family is a short discussion of basic genetics. Explain that when a baby is born, he has certain genes from each parent (and in turn from the parent's parent). These genes determine everything from height to eye color. Go as far as your child's interest on this takes you. Some kids are fascinated by dominant genes and heterozygous combinations. (Everyone has two genes for eye color, one from their mom and one from their dad. Your mom has blue eyes and your dad has brown. The brown gene is dominant, so why do you have blue eyes? Because your dad must be heterozygous—one brown and one blue gene, giving him brown eyes—and your mom must have two blue. You must have gotten your dad's blue gene along with one of your mom's blues. A blue and a blue equals blue. What if your dad was homozygous—two brown genes? Then no matter how many kids we had, all would have brown eyes.)

Use the genetic discussion to lead into a broader discussion. "If you can get eye color from an ancestor, do you think you could get courage, or musical ability, or a quick temper? What do you think you got from each of your grandparents?"

Spirit and Character

If you wish, carry the idea (and the discussion) one step further: "Son, if we can inherit all kinds of things from our parents and grandparents, is it possible we could also inherit something from our Heavenly Father—from God?"

Explain that all people have something called a conscience—something in their spirit that helps them know when something is right and when something is wrong. People who follow these feelings are happier—people who have the courage not to do something they sense is wrong, no matter how much pressure there is, and who dare to do what they feel is right even when it goes against the crowd.

Essential Element Nine: Practice (and Teach Kids) the Selective Use of Larger Institutions, and UNDERSTANDING of Today's Society

It may sound like a stretched or overdramatized analogy, but we need to think of (and teach our kids to perceive of) big institutions as similar to fire. Fire can warm, support, and sustain us, or it can consume and destroy us. Media and merchandising, business and banks, Internet and information are the same in this way—they can serve us or consume us. It's a lesson our parents and grandparents didn't need to teach us. It's a lesson we do need to teach our children and grandchildren.

They need to learn to perceive the world like our target diagram, with the family as the essence and the core, drawing on the outer sectors for support but never giving up their identity to them, never letting them replace or supplant family loyalty.

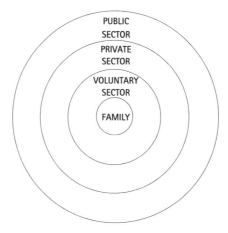

Children are capable, once they are seven or eight, of understanding this perspective, and can be taught to identify the larger institutions and know what each does to help us and what each does to hurt us. A parent can use a large version of the bull's-eye diagram and help a child fill in the big institutions that fit within each sector and list the good and bad effects that each can have on the family. Such a chart can serve as a "framework of warning" on what to avoid, from too-easy credit to overly expensive tastes, from media amorality to Internet pornography, from all-consuming employment to all-consuming recreation. If your children are older, go beyond the target diagram and share with them the charts that follow on pages 149 to 162, which will help them to understand the ten different types of large institutions that they should use selectively (accepting the good, rejecting the bad). Kids twelve and up will be able to think about and discuss some parts of these charts. The older they are, the more aspects of the charts they will find interesting.

The goal is not to make our kids paranoid or fearful in any way; it is to help them see the world as it really is. Children can become good critics who can see through advertising and promotion, who can recognize instant gratification for what it is, who can connect action to consequences whether others do or not, and most of all who can perceive the potential dangers stemming from the expansion instincts (and the greed) of larger institutions.

We'd been trying for months to help our kids see the world in the framework of the bull's-eye diagram and to be self-motivated critics of the materialism and amorality that lurk everywhere today. We had some indication that we were making progress when a child would say, "Yeah, sure," while watching a commercial on TV or would ask his friends if they knew how much a car really cost when you bought it on credit. We knew one of our boys had really mastered at least a part of it when he told us he'd found an Internet server he thought we should shift to because "it screens out all the garbage." But we really felt we were getting somewhere when we were driving our seventh-grade daughter home from a parent-teacher conference and she suddenly said, "You know, I've just got to go in and talk to my math teacher and tell him why I didn't think that test was fair. After all, he works for us!" We asked her what she meant, and she explained, "Well, we pay him, don't we? I mean, it's our taxes—he works for us. We own the schools. They don't own us. It's like you've been telling me—schools and stores and companies and stuff, even movies and music and the Internet, they shouldn't be telling us what to do. We should be telling them what to do!"

Well, we had to have a little discussion about the right and wrong ways to "tell them what to do," but we were delighted with her growing ability to think things through for herself and her capacity to be a critic rather than a pawnlike acceptor of everything.

The bottom line (and one that kids can understand and feel empowered by) is this: Live by your own values. Sift and screen the things the media and the schools and advertisements throw at you. Learn to recognize when a big institution's self-interests don't match up with your values, your beliefs, your sense of what's best for you and for your family. Most important of all, remember that while it is fine for a child (or for yourself) to feel certain loyalties to larger institutions, to their school, perhaps even to their favorite TV show or your favorite Internet site, your principal loyalty and allegiance should always be to the smallest institution—to your family! The review charts on the following pages can be helpful in going over with your child the pros and cons of each set of larger institutions.

1. Work/Professional Institutions

WHO	• The private sector, employers, corporate America.
GOOD SIDE *(family-beneficial)*	• Provides our income, our employment, and our professional identity.
BAD SIDE *(family-destructive)*	• Demands more and more time. • Causes disruptive relocations, dictated changes. • Kids raised by institutions other than family.
WHAT/HOW *(the essence of the problem)*	• Our jobs have become our identity more than our family. Too much mental energy as well as too much time is spent on work, too little on family. Being at work is easier (and gives us more recognition) than being at home.
FALSE PARADIGMS *(lies, false impressions, and self-justification)*	• "You are your work." • "Two incomes are almost always required to support a family." • "There are more rewards from work than from family."
ERRORS	A. KEY MISUSED WORDS • "Status" (meaning job title and income). • "Freedom" (meaning bondage now so that money will someday give you more options). B. LIFESTYLE MISTAKES • Giving work a higher priority than family. • Greed. C. BAD TRADE-OFFS • Things for time. • Work position for family position. • Job/company loyalty for family loyalty.

2. Financial Institutions

WHO	• Banks/credit unions/mortgage companies/credit cards/investment brokers.
GOOD SIDE *(family-beneficial)*	• Allows us to buy homes, earn on savings, etc. • Facilitates our physical care of families.
BAD SIDE *(family-destructive)*	• Makes credit problems too easy to come by. • Debt creates stress and takes away parents' time with kids. • The stress breaks up marriages.
WHAT/HOW *(the essence of the problem)*	• Easy credit spoils the work ethic. Families live beyond their means and then try to catch up by working excessive hours that rob family time and prioritize things above relationships.
FALSE PARADIGMS *(lies, false impressions, and self-justification)*	• "You deserve it—before you've earned it" (instant gratification). • "You need to 'have it all.' " • "All I want is the land next to mine."
ERRORS	**A. KEY MISUSED WORDS** • "Fulfillment" (meaning instant gratification). **B. LIFESTYLE MISTAKES** • Living beyond income. • Excess spending, insufficient saving. **C. BAD TRADE-OFFS** • Excess for balance. • Instant gratification for delayed gratification.

3. Merchandising Institutions

WHO	• Retail, advertising, marketing
GOOD SIDE *(family-beneficial)*	• Delivers needed goods and services to families.
BAD SIDE *(family-destructive)*	• Takes both time and money away from family. • Fosters materialism.
WHAT/HOW *(the essence of the problem)*	• There is too much out there—and advertising and merchandising are the fine art of making us think we need what we actually only want. Things get higher priorities than relationships.
FALSE PARADIGMS *(lies, false impressions, and self-justification)*	• "More is better." • "Instant gratification." • "You are what you own." • "He who dies with the most toys wins."
ERRORS	A. KEY MISUSED WORDS • "Needs" (meaning "wants"). • "Wealth" (meaning money and things). B. LIFESTYLE MISTAKES • Misuse of credit. • Living beyond means. C. BAD TRADE-OFFS • Work for family. • Money for time. • Gifts of things over gifts of time.

4. Entertainment and Media Institutions

WHO	• Movies, music, TV, radio.
GOOD SIDE *(family-beneficial)*	• Brings families together for shared experience. • Entertains us, "broadens" us, informs us, helps us communicate. • Can uplift, motivate, and inspire.
BAD SIDE *(family-destructive)*	• Takes time away from families. • Desensitizes us to violence, extramarital sex, divorce. • Creates false paradigms and surface-value systems.
WHAT/HOW *(the essence of the problem)*	• A small "cultural elite" of producers, directors, writers (500 or so) control virtually all of what we see and hear in media. Their hugely disproportionate influence allows this generally non-family-oriented minority to masquerade as a majority.
FALSE PARADIGMS *(lies, false impressions, and self-justification)*	• "Everyone does it." • "There are no consequences." • "We just reflect and report values and attitudes, we don't create or influence them." • Tolerance is the chief (perhaps the only) virtue. • Traditional values and traditional families are old-fashioned and unenlightened.
ERRORS	**A. KEY MISUSED WORDS** • "Love" (meaning lust). • "Adventure" (meaning violence). • "Tolerance" (meaning license). • "Wealth" (meaning money). • "News" meaning the spectacular and the negative.

B. PROMPTED LIFESTYLE MISTAKES

- Intimacy and cohabitation prior to marriage.
- Violent, win-lose conflict resolution.
- Divorce for convenience or whim.

C. BAD TRADE-OFFS

- Thrill for commitment.
- Self for family.

5. Information and Communication Institutions

WHO
- The Internet, telecommunication systems, data banks, and virtually endless access to information.

GOOD SIDE
(family-beneficial)
- Home can be source (allows more work to be done and therefore more time to be spent at home).

BAD SIDE
(family-destructive)
- Takes huge chunks of our time (takes it from family interaction).
- Pornography and violence only a click away.

WHAT/HOW
(the essence of the problem)
- Too much exposure to violence and all varieties of immoral and amoral behavior. Time wasted with superfluous information. Actual (virtual) interaction with destructive ideas, practices.

FALSE PARADIGMS
(lies, false impressions, and self-justification)
- "You're in touch."
- "Sex and violence are recreation."
- "Virtual reality is reality."

ERRORS

A. KEY MISUSED WORDS
- "In touch" (meaning "online" or informed but not touching people).
- "Important" (most of it isn't).
- "Connections" (but not *personal* ones).
- "Knowledge" (meaning information).

B. LIFESTYLE MISTAKES
- Sitting (virtual reality is not reality).

C. BAD TRADE-OFFS
- Cyberspace for real space.
- Information for wisdom.
- Information for common sense.

6. Political/Governmental Institutions

WHO	• All levels of executive and legislative government.
GOOD SIDE *(family-beneficial)*	• Protects us from outside aggression and from one another. Provides a safety net for those who can't help themselves.
BAD SIDE *(family-destructive)*	• "Marriage penalty" tax codes. • Oppressive taxes in general. • Welfare, which destroys initiative/responsibility.
WHAT/HOW *(the essence of the problem)*	• The "Big Brothers" of government attempt to control and substitute for families. Regulation, taxation, and welfare have all become "family-unfriendly."
FALSE PARADIGMS *(lies, false impressions, and self-justification)*	• "Bigger is better." • "Poverty causes values decline" (instead of the other way around). • "My private life affects only me." • "Nice guys finish last."
ERRORS	

A. KEY MISUSED WORDS
- "Equality" (meaning bringing everyone down to a common level).
- "Opportunity" (meaning conformity).
- "Benevolence" (meaning the destruction of initiative).

B. LIFESTYLE MISTAKES
- Depending on government rather than on ourselves and our families.

C. BAD TRADE-OFFS
- Security for agency.
- Dependence for independence.

7. *Educational Institutions*

WHO	• Preschools, primary and secondary schools, universities.
GOOD SIDE *family-beneficial)*	• Expands horizons, improves perspective. • Inspires, motivates. • Develops children's social and emotional capacities.
BAD SIDE *(family-destructive)*	• Doesn't teach values/character/discipline/responsibility (and parents think it does). • Takes over too much of child rearing, allowing parental abdication. • Separation of families (boarding schools).
WHAT/HOW *(the essence of the problem)*	• Schools become substitutes for families rather than supplements, trying to do things collectively for children (from teaching about sex to caring for them in after-school programs) that parents should do individually.
FALSE PARADIGMS *(lies, false impressions, and self-justification)*	• "You must have professional expertise to teach kids." • "Nurseries and preschools can handle kids better than parents." • "We can understand and explain everything scientifically."
ERRORS	**A. KEY MISUSED WORDS** • "Values-neutral" (meaning no values at all). • "Education" (meaning "imparting information"). **B. LIFESTYLE MISTAKES** • Trying to know more and more about less and less. • Turning over a child's present and future to the schools. **C. BAD TRADE-OFFS** • "Tolerance" for absolutes. • School responsibility for parental responsibility.

8. *Courts and Legal Institutions*

WHO
- Courts, judges, legal firms, lobbyists, litigators.

GOOD SIDE
(family-beneficial)
- Protection and rights, assets, persons.
- A way out for truly irreconcilable differences.

BAD SIDE
(family-destructive)
- Antifamily interpretation of law.
- Probate battles, custody battles, divorce battles.
- "Rights" become selfish demands that alienate family members from one another.

WHAT/HOW
(the essence of the problem)
- Legal "rights" and legal battles put individual needs and wants above family commitments and pit family members against one another, pulling family units apart. Judges put a higher priority on individual rights than they do on family commitments and obligations.

FALSE PARADIGMS
(false interests and self-justification)
- "The state knows more about what's good for children than parents."
- "It's better to escape problems than to resolve them."
- "If a marriage isn't good, admit your mistake and move on."
- "Kids are always better off with parents separating than staying together in conflict."

ERRORS

A. KEY MISUSED WORDS
- "Prenuptial agreement" (meaning tentative, conditional commitment).
- "Custody" (meaning win-lose).

B. LIFESTYLE MISTAKES
- Measuring success materially rather than matrimonially.

C. BAD TRADE-OFFS

- My needs for family needs.
- "Freedom" for responsibility.
- Money for relationships.
- Individual rights for family commitments.

9. Recreation and Social/Cultural Institutions

WHO	• Sports, arts, clubs, leagues, fast food, summer camps, rest homes, etc.
GOOD SIDE *(family-beneficial)*	• All can be participated in by families. • Many were created to assist and supplement families.
BAD SIDE *(family-destructive)*	• Parents don't teach kids directly ("subcontractor" approach). • Substitutes for family—takes place of family—make family seem unnecessary. • Takes the allegiance (and time) that should go to family. • Takes prime family time (Sundays, holidays, etc.). • Grandparents split off. • Families don't eat together or talk together.
WHAT/HOW *(the essence of the problem)*	• Social and cultural institutions substitute for families, and recreational institutions soak up family time.
FALSE PARADIGMS *(lies, false impressions, and self-justification)*	• "No time for kids . . . or for more kids." • "You owe yourself." (selfishness) • "If it feels good, do it." (hedonism) • "Sex is recreation."
ERRORS	A. KEY MISUSED WORDS • "Time-saving" (meaning time-wasting). • "Happiness" (meaning stretched too thin). • "The good life" (meaning overscheduled). • "Freedom" (meaning no commitment or responsibility). • "Accomplishment" (meaning I won, he lost).

B. LIFESTYLE MISTAKES

- "Subcontractor" approach to parenting (others will do the specifics of teaching my kids).

C. BAD TRADE-OFFS

- Friends for children.
- Friends for parents.
- Physical for spiritual.
- Group traditions for family traditions.

10. Religious Institutions (in decline)
Self-Help/Psychiatric Help (fast growth)

WHO	• Churches/synagogues/mosques.
	• Analysts/seminars/infomercials/gurus.
GOOD SIDE *(family-beneficial)*	• Can promote faith, values.
	• Can instruct, help, and supplement families.
BAD SIDE *(family-destructive)*	• Churches not taking strong stands on what is right.
	• Churches not providing enough chances to serve.
	• Loss of worship, of faith. Substituted for by self-help.
WHAT/HOW *(the essence of the problem)*	• Too many churches have been irrelevant bystanders in the decline of values and the disintegration of families. Instead of faith, we've begun to rely on pop self-help ideas to bring us happiness and fulfillment.
FALSE PARADIGMS *(lies, false impressions, and self-justification)*	• "Situational morality."
	• "Customized values."
	• Religion is self-righteous, self-serving, and strident."
	• I'm number one.
ERRORS	A. KEY MISUSED WORDS
	• "Control" (meaning there should be no surprises).
	• "Independence" (meaning "needing no one").
	• "Crutch" (meaning you shouldn't need anyone).
	B. LIFESTYLE MISTAKES
	• Nothing sacred (God's name, God's day, etc.).

C. BAD TRADE-OFFS

- "Tolerance" for absolutes.
- Self-confidence for faith.
- Short-term for long-term.
- Easier quick-fix happiness for harder long-term joy.

Summary of Solution Two (Elements 5, 6, 7, 8, and 9)

There is a very direct solution for the problem of larger institutions that undermine families and assume too many of the roles and functions that traditionally belonged to families. The solution is simply to create a family institution that is so involving, so binding, so security- and identity-giving that it supersedes and overwhelms the influence of any other institution, no matter how big. Creating strong family rules, family traditions, family heritage, and a family economy does exactly this.

On top of it all, parents can consciously teach their children to recognize the negative and the positive influences of big media, big business, big advertising, and big government, helping them learn to use and enjoy the good even as they reject or ignore the bad.

The beauty of proactive parenting is that parents set the agenda and the priorities. The "bull's-eye" of family becomes the true center and focal point, and the outer community private and public rings take their proper place as supporters and protectors of the family. When parents create bull's eye families, children come out secure and well grounded, and they welcome later opportunities to care for the parents who cared for them.

Create a Pattern for

Teaching Correct Principles

and Basic Values

While they may be "natural" and full of common sense, there is nothing automatic about correct principles and basic values. There is no guarantee that your children will absorb from you the truths and basic moral judgments that you'd like to pass on to them. In today's world, it truly is a battle for the hearts and minds of our children. Their minds and personalities, so open and susceptible, are courted by the media and by the peer group and by every large organization or company that would like to add them to their following or to their "customer base." As we've suggested, children begin essentially as "values vacuums"—they will suck in whatever they are exposed to most strongly and most frequently.

As parents, we must be both proactive and preemptive in teaching correct principles and basic values to our children. The principles, values, identity, and self-image we establish in them not only influence the decisions they make and the type of lives they live; they form a social and spiritual "immune system" that shields and protects them from the false paradigms and antivalues that can undermine their chances for long-term happiness.

The final two "essential elements" are what build this spiritual immune system and give children an identity strong enough to withstand the negative and self-destructive illusions that they are more exposed to than any other generation of kids that has ever lived.

Essential Element Ten:
Substitute Correct PRINCIPLES for False Paradigms

It's a family challenge that no other era of parents and spouses have faced: *how to undo or supersede the damage and danger of widespread and pervasive false paradigms.* No earlier families had to face a world where a media minority masqueraded so successfully as a majority, where materialism and instant gratification were the accepted norms, and where conditional morality and selfish expediency had pretty much overthrown the ideas of absolutes and of spiritual sources of good and evil.

False paradigms have a way of getting in our heads and of staying there until we replace them with something better and truer. As parents, it's hard to overcome the "bacteria" that come at us from the world if our immune systems are weakened by false paradigms. And children, literally surrounded and bombarded by the false world views, are not going to recognize them, let alone reject them, unless we give them sound replacements.

But forget trying to replace false paradigms in kids' heads before we have corrected them in our own. An attitude or a paradigm manifests itself in all sorts of ways—obvious and subtle—and there is no way to fake it. So we need to correct ourselves first.

The most straightforward way to overcome and slip out of the clutches and influence of false paradigms is to openly *assert* your belief in their exact opposites. Do whatever you have to do—make a chart of correct principles, of things as they really are, of what you believe, and hang it on your wall, or put it in a family mission statement or make a screen saver out of it for your personal computer. Find your own way to pledge your allegiance to some simple, clear, positive principles that will cut through the smoke screen of the prevailing false paradigms.

There are five basic, true principles that can be taught within a family. They are the exact antithesis of the five false paradigms we listed earlier, and they can set up a foundation on which a strong family can be maintained and strong individual lives can be lived. They will "ring true" to you as you read them, because deep within ourselves we are recognizers of truth. Notice, as they are discussed, how directly they counter and correct the false paradigms created by the media and by popular culture that were outlined earlier. (Turn back to page 82 and notice that the first correct principle is the exact opposite of the first false paradigm, etc.)

Principle 1—The Opposite of Paradigm Problem 1 (see page 82): Families Are Essential, Important, and Irreplaceable. They Do Five Things that Nothing Else Can Do.

It's so easy to *assume* that our children know how important families are. After all, they are part of a family, they came into the world through a family, and they are dependent on their family every day of their young lives. But they live in a world that gives so little credit or recognition to families! It's so easy for them to take their own family for granted and to get the idea that the slices of life they get from media could go on and get along fine without families.

So the thing to do is to teach them otherwise. One of the most effective ways to communicate the essential roles or functions of families is through a simple game (this will work with and interest a child eight or older):

1. Number a blank sheet of paper down the left-hand side, one through five.

2. Ask the child how many things he can think of that only a family can do. Give "clues" until he gets each one (see page 83). They

will come in a child's vocabulary, which is fine ("have kids," "make us happy," "teach us what's right," etc.).

3. Challenge each one. Say, "Well, what if they could make babies in test tubes—would that be good? Why not?" Or "Well, we can learn what's right in church or school, too—isn't that just as good?"

4. Praise and reward a child for his participation and his answers. Then tell him *your* beliefs in the importance of families and your feelings on why only families can do the best job on any of those five important jobs.

Principle 2—The Opposite of Paradigm Problem 2 (see page 84): The Spiritual Majority Is Always on the Side of What Is Right.

Whether you count angels in your interpretation of that, or whether it's just a question of the "might" that goes with right, it's a truth that you can rely on and that you can teach to your children. Here are two things kids need to know in order to accept and live by this principle (each can be discussed with and taught to children eight and older):

A. The facts run contrary to the implication of most movies, TV shows, and rock songs:

- Premarital sex is *not* the norm—and there *are* consequences. Slightly more than half of high school students are virgins. And half of those who have had sex say they wish they hadn't.

- The F word is *not* the most commonly used word in the English language.

- Everyone worth knowing does *not* drive a trendy new car, wear only name brands, and live in luxury.

- Divorce is *not* something that happens smoothly and easily and without long-term problems or consequences.

- People still value commitments and relationships and character.

B. Most of what we see on the large and small screen and hear in popular music comes directly from a small and nonrepresentative subculture—a few hundred people who produce and direct and decide on most of what comes to us as media and entertainment. Most of this group are neither as family-oriented nor as religiously inclined as the average American. It is they, not we, who are the minority. But their visibility and influence, magnified a million times by media, make them appear as a majority.

Kids who understand these simple facts will have an immunity of sorts to the compelling "be part of it" influence of media. They will be able to stand aside a bit and see error as error, figure consequences for actions, and take some comfort in the fact that what they believe is more common than it sometimes seems.

Principle 3—The Opposite of Paradigm Problem 3 (see page 88): What Matters Is What's Inside, What You've Worked for and Waited for, and What You Give.

The world whispers to us (sometimes shouts) that what matters is:

A. Outside appearances.

B. Instant gratification.

C. How much we can get.

Yet we know, almost all of us know, that these are not only delusions, they are directly opposite-of-truth lies. What really matters is:

A. Who and what we are inside.

B. Good things worked for (and often waited for), especially relationships.

C. How much we can give.

In surveys, substantial majorities say that family is more important than possessions, character than appearance. Yet in so many ways we believe in one creed and live by another. When the current goes one way, it takes strong swimming to move in the other. There is real determination and effort required to get to and stay with a place that society seems to be moving away from.

Sometimes the key is as simple as reminding ourselves of who we are and what we believe. And reminding ourselves that the real majority still believes with us. As we remind ourselves, we must teach our children. "What matters" is a topic and a discussion that can't come up too often.

Principle 4—The Opposite of Paradigm Problem 4 (see page 90): Joy Comes from Commitment, Sacrifice, and Delayed Gratification.

Like any true principle, this one is truly learned and truly taught only by living it. But along with the living should come the straightforward telling. We need to tell our children boldly and clearly that the whole hedonistic approach of seeking happiness through pleasure and self-gratification is a crock.

> I was on a several-hour drive one summer with my son from our house to a vacation destination. In his early adolescence, he seemed so vulnerable and influenceable by everything around him. He wanted to wear the right brands, to have the things that "everyone else" had, to try out and feel everything, right or wrong, that his friends were telling him about. And he wanted to have and be and try all of it now. I wanted to use the drive time to talk him out of some of this and convince him of the value of commitment, sacrifice, and delayed gratification, but I knew a lecture on my theories wouldn't cut it.
>
> The only other one in the car with us was our chocolate Labrador dog, and we were talking about her. My son loved the dog and was interested in animals and biology in general. It was a safe subject. Somehow we got from what we were talking about to what I wanted to talk about. Instinct and appetites, we decided, are what make animals accomplish their purposes and find their happiness. Following those instincts, urges, and appetites allows them to stay alive, reproduce, and keep the whole biological ecosystem balanced and functional. What makes humans different from animals was that we get our happiness and maximize our potential not by following but by controlling our

appetites. Animals' appetites control them. Humans must control their appetites. Then we talked about various appetites—for food, for sex, for possessions, for recognition. I was amazed at how clearly my fourteen-year-old could see how each of those appetites, if allowed to control us, could hurt us and cause unhappiness to ourselves and others. But I was even more impressed that he could see how controlling them could make us better and happier.

So much of our world feeds us and our children the disastrous hedonistic attitudes of pleasure-seeking and instant gratification—an animalistic philosophy. We also get bombarded with the notion that "freedom" and "commitment" are opposites, that loyalties to family relationships "tie us down" and cause us to want. By our example and our words, we must help our children see how big this lie is. We must try both to teach and to exemplify its opposite.

Principle 5—The Opposite of Paradigm Problem 5 (see page 92): Absolute Right and Absolute Help Both Exist and Both Can Be Reached.

More than 90 percent of Americans believe in God.[24] And while the specifics of belief vary widely, most accept many of the same connected convictions about the nature of the Deity and about the eternal nature of their own soul or spirit. Although there are many different faiths, when it comes to the basics, various world religions could almost be interpreted by an outside analyst as a game of how many different ways there are to say the same things. Most beliefs of believers are virtually universal:

God exists, lives.

He is our Father/Creator.

God is good—the ultimate good.

He gives truth about how we should live (in Scripture, etc.).

But He respects our agency (allows us to choose).

He hears and answers prayers and gives guidance.

He can forgive and we can improve.

We have within us a spirit or soul that continues after death.

It is important to see and understand the *ramifications* of belief in God and in a life hereafter—to see what it should mean in terms of our general view of life and our rejection of paradigms and attitudes that are inconsistent with spiritual beliefs.

A. God is the *source* of good, so His principles *define* what is right. (If there were no God, it could be argued that any set of principles would be as good as any other.)

B. Therefore, *absolutes* exist. God's word or way and what leads to it is absolutely good and what leads away from it is absolutely bad.

C. A belief in God and in absolutes can simplify life in a positive way, giving us a framework of what is right and wrong, good and bad, relieving us of the oppressive obligation to make every one of those judgments for ourselves.

Beliefs and absolutes are the key to knowing who we are and to understanding life's purpose. If God is the father, we are the children. If He is the owner and giver, then we are the receivers and stewards. If He loves us, then there is positive purpose in being born into and living through mortality, and there is ongoing life and additional opportunity beyond death. How we live and what we learn here will affect who and what we are there.

This eternal perspective makes life more beautiful as well as more meaningful. Our faith allows us to perceive ourselves as:

- Sons and daughters of (or at least creations of) God.
- Recipients of the gift of this mortality: physical bodies on a physical earth—sent to the perfect school/laboratory on earth, where there are many options and possibilities.
- Choosers of good or evil; self-determining.
- Beings capable of love, which precipitates happiness.
- Able to make commitments and create families, wherein lie life's deepest joy.
- Subject to God's commandments (the most important of which involve the taking and the starting of life), which are best viewed as "loving counsel from a wise Father."

- Capable of returning to God, of continuing to live and progress in an afterlife.

What do we do with these beliefs, shared by a majority but talked about too seldom? The best thing to do is to *remind* ourselves and our children of what we believe . . . and of the reality and consistency of what is right and what is wrong . . . and of the need we all have for help from God . . . and of the happiness that runs so parallel with goodness. We need to remind ourselves and our children often enough and strongly enough that those reminders outweigh the opposite (counterfeit) messages of the world.

Perhaps the best reminder of all is prayer. Most people pray, but too often only sporadically or in times of particular need. Remember that family prayer or prayer with children at bedtime or before a meal, in addition to whatever spiritual help it may bring, is a powerful statement to your child that you believe, that there are absolutes, and that we don't have to depend entirely on ourselves.

Teaching these five correct principles within your family is no easy (or quick) matter. Remember that they are the very opposites of what the broader culture is trying to teach your children. You must undertake living them and teaching them with commitment and consistency. A good way to start is by making them *visible* in your home. Try putting together a simple chart or poster that could go on a wall in your family room or kitchen.

Principles

1. Families do five things that no one else can do.

2. The spiritual majority is always on the side of what's right.

3. What matters is what's inside, what you've worked and waited for, and what you give.

4. Joy comes from commitment, sacrifice, and delayed gratification.

5. Absolute right and absolute help both exist.

If your children are under eight, the chart will be mostly for you—to remind you of the example you want to set and to make you more aware of situations that may arise that give you small opportunities to talk about one of the principles with one of your small children. With children eight or older, the chart or poster can be a focal point for little family meetings or dinnertime discussions. You can ask what each of the five principles means, what examples children can think of, and further subquestions about each of the five principles.

As the principles become more familiar to your children, you will have a "framework" within which you can discuss little everyday things that either support or go against any of the principles—a TV ad that promotes instant gratification, a song with lyrics suggesting that everybody cheats, a situation with friends who have different rules or standards.

Find your own ways of establishing and emphasizing these five principles, which counter the five false paradigms, and you will have acquired for your family the tenth essential element!

Essential Element Eleven:
"VALUES Therapy" to Build a Self-Image for Life

Parents, today more than ever, need clear and specific goals and plans for their families. We need an offense good enough that we're not forced to constantly react and to rely always on our defense. The best offense in today's world is a plan for teaching our children values that will protect them, maximize their chances to be happy, and avoid some of the problems for which you would need more defense. Even beyond the five true principles of Element 10, children need a full array of solid, time-tested values.

In researching and writing an earlier book, Teaching Your Children Values, *we sought twelve values, one for each month of the year, that were truly universal, that virtually all parents everywhere would desire for their child and that, together, would create the kind of character in a child that would maximize his chance for a happy and productive life. We surveyed and questioned parents and came up with this list:*

1. HONESTY: *Truthfulness with other individuals, with institutions, with society, with self. The inner strength and confidence that is bred by exacting truthfulness, trustworthiness, and integrity.*

2. COURAGE: *Daring to attempt difficult things that are good. Strength not to follow the crowd, to say no and mean it and influence others by it. Being true to convictions and following good impulses even when they are unpopular or inconvenient. Boldness to be outgoing and friendly.*

3. PEACEABLENESS: *Calmness, peacefulness, serenity. The tendency to try to accommodate rather than argue. The understanding that differences are seldom resolved through conflict and that meanness in others is an indication of their problem or insecurity and thus of their need for your understanding. The ability to understand how others feel rather than simply reacting to them. Control of temper.*

4. SELF-RELIANCE AND POTENTIAL: *Individuality. Awareness and development of gifts and uniqueness. Taking responsibility for own actions. Overcoming the tendency to blame others for difficulties. Commitment to personal excellence.*

5. SELF-DISCIPLINE AND MODERATION: *Physical, mental, and financial self-discipline. Moderation in speaking, in eating, in exercising. The controlling and bridling of one's own appetites. Understanding the limits of body and mind. Avoiding the dangers of extreme, unbalanced viewpoints. The ability to balance self-discipline with spontaneity.*

6. FIDELITY AND CHASTITY:

The value and security of fidelity within marriage and of restraint and limits before marriage. The commitments that go with marriage and that should go with sex. A grasp of the long-range (and widespread) consequences that can result from casual, recreational sex and from infidelity.

7. LOYALTY AND DEPENDABILITY:

Loyalty to family and to employers, country, church, schools, and other organizations and institutions to which commitments are made. Support, service, contribution. Reliability and consistency in doing what you say you will do.

8. RESPECT:

Respect for life, for property, for parents, for elders, for nature, and for the beliefs and rights of others. Courtesy, politeness, and manners. Self-respect and the avoidance of self-criticism.

9. LOVE:

Individual and personal caring that goes both beneath and beyond loyalty and respect. Love for friends, neighbors, even adversaries. And a prioritized, lifelong commitment of love for family.

10. UNSELFISHNESS AND SENSITIVITY:

Becoming more other-centered and less self-centered. Learning to feel with and for others. Empathy, tolerance, brotherhood. Sensitivity to needs in people and situations.

11. KINDNESS AND FRIENDLINESS:

Awareness that being kind and considerate is more admirable than being tough or strong. The tendency to understand rather than confront. Gentleness, particularly toward those who are younger or weaker.

	The ability to make and keep friends. Help-fulness. Cheerfulness.
12. JUSTICE AND MERCY:	*Obedience to law, fairness in work and play. An understanding of natural consequences and the law of the harvest. A grasp of mercy and forgiveness and an understanding of the futility (and bitter poison) of carrying a grudge.*

There are all kinds of simple and effective methods, techniques, stories, games, and other ideas to teach each of these values to kids,* but the most important and overriding method is simply to focus and concentrate on one single value each month, to make it the "value of the month" in your family and to look for opportunities (in everything from the media you watch to the everyday situations you find yourself in) to talk about it and to point it out to your child. Assign one value to each month and, when the year ends, start over (for example, your eight-year-old is now nine and will learn each value on a new level). Here is our family's list:

January:	Honesty
February:	Courage
March:	Peaceableness
April:	Self-Reliance and Potential
May:	Self-Discipline and Moderation
June:	Fidelity and Chastity
July:	Loyalty and Dependability
August:	Respect
September:	Love

---

* A special program of twelve monthly audiotape sets is now available. Each set (one for each value) contains a parent's tape of methods, stories, games, and other ideas to teach that value to different-age children and a child's tape (called *Alexander's Amazing Adventures*), by which kids learn the value vicariously via an imaginative and musical adventure story. See the Closing section of this book for more information or visit valuesparenting.com.

October: Unselfishness and Sensitivity

November: Kindness and Friendliness

December: Justice and Mercy

Properly approached, this "values offense" is not some burden of "one more thing to worry about." Quite the contrary—it's a simplifier. It gives a parent one clear subject to concentrate on for the month rather than worrying about everything at once. It's not a panacea, and it's not something that has to be worked on every day, but when you've got a minute, when you find yourself with a child in the car or in the kitchen, you mention the value, you work on it *with* them. Just defining the words and talking about the value helps. You comment on your own need for it, quest for it, problems with it, and so forth, and the effect is cumulative. A little better each month, a little better each year, building a base of shared and understood values that becomes a lifetime defense against the false paradigms and larger institutions that threaten to swallow up our children and our families.

There is one method that has, for our family, been a way of bringing all twelve of the values together and seeking practical application of them in our children's lives. We call it "making decisions in advance," and it works like this:

1. *During the first two or three years of elementary school (ages five to seven), we try to talk a lot with a child about decisions—about how much fun they can be and how important they are. We also use the word* consequences *a lot and help the child see how* consequences *are tied to decisions. We try to let him make as many decisions as possible for himself—anything from which shirt to wear to which kind of juice to have for breakfast.*

2. *When the child is eight, at the back of his journal or diary (something every child should have), have him write the headline "Decisions I Have Already Made." Then we talk about two kinds of big decisions—the ones you can't make until you know all your options and are older (college, marriage, profession, etc.) and the ones that are actually best made*

in advance (whether to do drugs, whether to cheat on tests, whether to smoke, etc.).

3. *Even when the child understands, we ask him to wait—not to write down any "decisions in advance" just yet but to think about it for a week or two. Then, at another "meeting," when we're not rushed and really have some time, we ask the child if he has any decisions in advance that he wants to write in the special place at the back of his journal. We explain that when he writes it, he should sign his signature by it and date it, so it's like a contract or promise to himself.*

4. *When he comes up with one, we say, in essence, "Wait. Before you write it and sign it, let us tell you a story about what might happen to you in a few years." Then we try to create the most difficult possible scenario for the decision he's proposed. For example, if he's said his decision in advance is never to do drugs, we'll have him imagine he's at a party when he's sixteen and a group of his friends want him to try a pill. "Come on. We've all taken one—they make you feel great." The girl he's with takes one. Everyone's looking at him. What does he do? What does he say? If he feels sure he could handle the situation, we say, "Great. Now I think you're ready to list it and sign it."*

   As we've done this over the years with our children, almost every value has come into play. It is a way for them to commit themselves to the practical and future application of each value. It works well with seven- to eleven-year-olds, but we think eight is the very best age to start. The list can be added to for years as they come to other conclusions and commitments. It's not a panacea or a guarantee, but it increases a child's chances of making good choices for years to come.

We call this whole-values approach "values therapy" because we have observed what a healing, security-giving, therapeutic effect it has on children. Kids who understand basic values (well enough to incorporate them mentally into their concept of who they are) develop strong, healthy self-images and self-esteem.

The ancient Greeks had a word for the cultivation of character, values, and virtue in a child. The word was *paideia*. Whatever we call it, it is something that can be done, and doing it can make all the difference for your child. Adopting a "value of the month" approach can have a powerful and therapeutic effect on your children and can make your family the possessor of the eleventh essential element.

Summary of Solution 3 (Elements 10 and 11)

The false paradigms and antivalues that pervade today's world and that trouble all concerned parents do not yield to a defensive or corrective approach. We can't wait or be content just to watch for negative values or dangerous or false perspectives to crop up in our children and then try to correct them. Parents today must make preemptive strikes, winning over the minds and hearts of their own children and instilling basic values and correct principles in a purposeful and proactive way so that our children's brains and spirits are full enough of the good stuff that there's not much room left for the bad.

What we have going for us is that kids are instinctive and intuitive *recognizers* of truth. They like the feeling they get when they think about simple, basic values, and they like even more the worth and satisfaction they get when they make a right choice and get recognized and praised for it by their parents.

As you embark on an organized approach to teaching your children correct principles and basic values, you will find the personal satisfaction that you are maximizing their chance to bypass major mistakes and to find an essentially happy life.

CLOSING

Society, Support Groups, and the Twelfth

Element

After You Do All You Can Do

The eleven elements just outlined are the best ways we know for an individual family to counter, within itself, the family-destructive influences of today's world. Parents who make serious attempts at each of these eleven elements will protect and preserve their own families and maximize their children's chances of a happy, productive life and of strong families of their own.

If they are the best ideas for *individual* families, what are the best ideas for *collective* families? Can parents band together in some effective way and persuade larger institutions to do more to help families and less to hurt them?

Maybe so. In this closing, we will try to make the case for serious revaluing of families by all sectors of our society, along with some possibilities for your involvement on a broader scale—in a parent's "movement" that might be hard for larger institutions to ignore. Finally, we will suggest a twelfth essential element—one that can help you work more effectively in your own family and within the broader society.

Said another way: Part Two has outlined the short-term solution for individual families. And it is the short term that parents should be most interested in. Parenting is a short-term proposition. We have a child in our home for only about eighteen years, and the needs kids have and the problems they face are *now*. Parenting is not "quick fix," but it is short-term!

Remember this, however: Parents are also the consumers, the managers, and the decision makers of the broader society, and while the short-term solutions have to do with what can happen in our homes, the long-term solutions for both families and society have to do with the changes parents can encourage in the broader society.

Somewhere in between the short-term "micro" solutions in our homes and the long-term "macro" solutions in our society, there is a middle ground that helps in both directions. By finding support groups in our neighborhoods or churches, we create the kind of "villages" that help us raise our own children and at the same time we become organized in a way that increases our chances of making the larger institutions around us more responsive and more supportive of the family.

SHORT TERM (Micro)	MIDDLE GROUND FINDING FAMILY SUPPORT	LONG TERM (Macro)
Solutions in our own homes (the 11 essential elements)	Groups to supplement individual families and to prod larger institutions	Solutions in our society (more family sensitivity and support from larger institutions)

In this closing, we will briefly address ways in which we hope the outer rings in our diagram (page 44) will become more supportive and responsive to the bull's-eye, and then suggest specific ways that you can build a support group that will first of all help with your own family and with the raising of your own children and then perhaps help to push and prod larger institutions to do more for families. Finding or building such a support group is so important that we call it the Twelfth Essential Element.

Society (a Parent's Plea)

Stronger individual families are the short-term solution! And the solution is possible and available in every home in America. But fixing our own families doesn't mean we can't also cry out to the culture that surrounds us, asking all parts of it to stop any practice or policy that threatens families and to start giving us more help in raising the children that are everyone's future.

Right now, as we've discussed, the larger institutions of our society, as they pursue their own preservation and expansion, are undermining, superseding, and otherwise destroying the basic institution of the family in a hundred ways. Every part of society—from banks to businesses, from media to manufacturers, and from government agencies to news agencies to ad agencies—must come to realize that as they weaken and undermine families they are ultimately destroying themselves. None of them can exist without the foundation of stable households that are the demand engine and the end consumer of every good or service that they produce and provide. The survival of all the large institutions we have created depends entirely on the survival of solid individual households and families.

Some argue otherwise: Who needs families? they say. Individuals are consumers, individuals are employees, individuals are what make up society. Who cares if they are married or if they live together as families?

Statistics and common sense provide the answer. Married individuals earn more, produce more, and consume more than single individuals—30 percent more. Try to imagine any business school or government surviving a 30 percent decline in sales, in production, or in tax base. And try to imagine a society reproducing and successfully raising its work force and its consumer base without functional, nurturing families.

Parents provide a huge service to society by raising its next generation, its next work force, its next taxpayers, its next universe of consumers. Current estimates of the cost of raising a child to age eighteen are around $150,000. Yet we do little to repay families. In fact, there are punishments ranging from higher taxes to job and career disadvantages.

In earlier times, children were an economic advantage to parents—they helped on the farm and with the other manual labor of households. Today children are a huge economic drain on their parents and neither government nor business does much to ease the burden or support the effort. The bottom line is that we all depend on families. And as surely as we depend on them individually, we depend on them institutionally.

When larger institutions have policies or practices that weaken or harm families, it is almost always a classic example of trading long-term viability for short-term gains. It is a macro example of choosing instant gratification over permanent stability.

- A bank makes credit too easy and increases short-term profits but generates bankruptcies and family financial instability that diminish the bank's long-term deposits and profits.

- A business down-sizes and reduces family-related benefits and thus raises its current income, but it suffers in the long run because it loses employee loyalty, morale, and stability.

- A movie focuses on violence and irresponsible, recreational sex and produces a box office hit on a relatively low budget. But life imitates art, and kids make mistakes that hurt themselves economically as well as emotionally, and theaters as well as every other part of commerce eventually pay the price.

- A TV news show focuses on the seamy and the shocking and gives much more attention to "alternative lifestyles" than to family lifestyle. Curiosity and titillation help the Nielsen rating but undermine the families that we're counting on to provide the next generation of viewers.

- A merchandiser/advertiser disguises wants as needs, helping create a narcissistic, hedonistic society of instant gratification. People buy more and product companies earn more in the short term, but at the expense of family stability and long-term prosperity, both in households and in businesses.

- A business refuses the options of flex time, job sharing, and maternity leave in the name of avoiding disruption and inconvenience but ends up losing some of its most competent employees, who decide to put family first.

- A neighborhood sports team (or a college or pro league) decides to schedule more of its games on Sunday to increase attendance but makes parents choose between sports and family time or church time, eventually weakening families and undermining future community support for the team.

- A legislature creates a marriage tax penalty (makes it so a married couple is taxed more than the same two individuals living or filing separately). It increases short-term tax reserves but undermines the family's ability to raise the next generation's tax base.

- A high school teaches every imaginable class related to career and occupation but pays no attention to family or parenting skills or to ethics. Kids are prepared to go out and get a job but not to raise the kids or establish the home that will support and supply the school and the general economy.

- A law firm encourages and supports and recommends divorce as the common solution, lining their pockets with fees but splitting up the families that constitute the communities in which they exist.

Before we get to the things larger institutions should start doing for families, we should all conclude that the first order of business is to get them to stop doing things that hurt families. *Stopping* the things that work against an ideal is always the best way to *start* pursuing that ideal.

We once attended a church congregation where the lay bishop was, by profession, a plumber. Despite his lack of training, he did his best to counsel and advise his parishioners. In the same congregation was a high-priced, highly educated therapist/psychiatrist who had many congregation members as his paying clients. But on several occasions people had dropped him as their doctor and therapist, reporting that the plumber/bishop was helping them more. Finally, in frustration, the therapist went to the bishop and asked him his secret. *"How do you, without any training, help people more than I do? What do you tell them to do?"*

The bishop gave a typically blunt and simple answer: "It's what I tell them not to do," he said. "I just ask them questions until I figure out which of the commandments they are breaking. Then I tell them to stop it."

Similarly, the first message we need to get to larger institutions is "stop it." Stop undermining and sabotaging the family! Put an end to any policies or practices that weaken or threaten families in any way.

We were featured guest speakers not long ago at Michael Eisner's convention of top Disney corporate officers and division heads. We wrote a brief statement that we called "A Parent's Plea" for the occasion, attempting to articulate the appeal we felt all parents would want to extend to the Disney organization in light of some of their moves away from the family entertainment that had been their historical hallmark.

A PARENT'S PLEA

We appeal to you now, today, as parents, as "everyparent," from a part of the heart that only parents know. We have been with you in these convention sessions, looked around, and tried to calculate the influence in this room. It reaches every American and every American child and beyond—to the whole world, not periodically but daily.

Because of your size and who you are, because of media's stretch and subtle stimulus, you may have more influence than any other company, even more, perhaps, than any other single institution of any kind, more than the presidency, more than the Congress. Actually, influence is too small a word. You have stewardship. You touch our children every day. They listen to you longer and with more concentration than to us.

What we say to you now is born not of statistical analysis or profit-margin expertise (although we promise you that goodness sells). It comes from a simple clarity bestowed only on parents. Because, you see, while our own personal commitments and values, our desires and dreams may quiver with ambiguity, they take on a firm, sharp focus in what we want for our children. As mere people, we are confused by complexity when we look at our world. But as parents, we are touched by simple pure wisdom when we look at our child. In that wisdom, we see the joy of right decisions, the wonder and trust of selfless love, and the nobility of simple courage. We see the good and love in the world reflected in our children's eyes. We feel the deep desire to pour all that is good into their lives. And we feel the need for help because we also see the damning dangers of the dark dimming of sensitivity, the callous desensitizing and loss of wonder that not only robs them of their childhood but steals their awe and hope.

So, first, we thank you for the times you have portrayed the light better and stronger than others portray the dark (and when you portray the dark for showing it accurately, for making it lose), for the times when you have reached the deeper realism of right that is truly stronger than might. Thank you for escapes into fantasy that are not to places outside ourselves, but to the deepest and truest parts of our own hearts. Thank you for the times you've shown the courage to speak of and to the spirit and softly and carefully of a higher, better being to go with a higher, better way. Thanks for the times you have avoided mindless amorality, which is, in its public face, more widely destructive than immorality.

Media, goes the old poppycock, doesn't influence a society's values, it only reflects them. Is that why prime-time ads cost a million a minute—to reflect? Media influences us and our children so profoundly it cannot be measured. "With influence comes responsibility" goes the old cliché. A stewardship? A burden to bear? But isn't it more an opportunity, an opportunity to lift, to love, to help us all live in a higher realm?

As parents, our plea to you is so basic: Help us. Help us remind ourselves and our children of who we really are and who we really can be. Help us to see the light within ourselves. Help us to be better parents by being our ally, by giving our children heroes and models, by creating good that is both beautiful and believable.

If you err, err toward the light. Be willing to earn a 15 percent instead of a 20 percent profit by avoiding the dark. Light brings strength, and a surefooted, clearheaded creativity and confidence that make up (financially and otherwise) much more than the missing 5 percent. Err to the light, not only in turning down a bribe, or a sweatshop, or a tax dodge. Err to the light in turning down an amoral script, or a superfluous excess of unacceptable language or violence, or a tarnishing sit-com. Err to the light in telling the story of the noble human spirit rather than the pseudo-sophisticated "realism" of the underside. Err to the light by believing and portraying that human beings are still good at their core.

From parents to Disney: Err on the side of right, err on the side of light.

The same kind of parent's plea could be made to all larger institutions. "Remember who you serve. Remember that strong families are your base and foundation. Be more aware of how your policies and practices affect families. Stop doing things that hurt families. Start doing more things that help families."

Recommendations to Larger Institutions
(Extending the Parent's Plea)

We must keep in mind that none of our new, large institutions consciously intends to damage or weaken families—at least not directly. But the goal of their own preservation and expansion occupies them and is not consciously or conceptually tied to the necessity of the strong family base. It is that *consciousness* of mutual dependency that we need more of in our larger institutions. If it were possible to wave a magic wand and change one thing, the most productive wave would be to cause the policymakers of every larger institution to be more aware of and feel responsible for the impact of their actions and policies on families. This one focus, this one awareness ("How does what we are doing impact families?"), could literally change the world and protect and preserve our society by saving and preserving our foundation of real homes and stable households.

It is interesting (and almost inspirational) to imagine each of the other sectors operating with the conscious goal of supporting, strengthening, and bolstering the family. In this vision, the outer rings transform and revitalize themselves by returning to their original purpose of serving and protecting the bull's-eye.

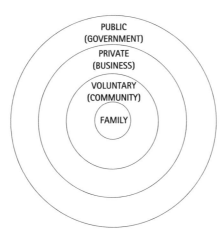

The Vision

1. *Community and Voluntary Ring:* Neighborhood organizations and churches teach parenting skills and orient every auxiliary, from scouting to Little League, toward family participation and involvement. Ministers take strong stands for marriage partners' staying together and for restraint and responsible sexual behavior among youth. Civic clubs focus on helping and supplementing families, and service organizations encourage parents and children to volunteer together to help other families. Extended families and genealogical societies work to give members a sense of roots and heritage.

2. *Private Sector (Business) Ring:* Employers adopt family-friendly policies for maternity and paternity leave, for transfer practices, for flex time and job sharing, and even for education and elder-care assistance (policies that are more profitable over the long run anyway). Marketers and advertisers replace the themes of self-fulfillment and instant gratification with a slant toward the

warmth and joy of family and commitment (a tone that sells better anyway). Media creators, producers, and participants opt for themes of love and loyalty and the striving for family solidarity rather than the obsession with greed, sleaze, and dysfunctionality (approaches that ultimately draw more viewers and sell more tickets anyway).

3. *Public Sector (Government) Ring:* Every policy, law, judgment, and priority is weighted by the question, "Is the family served?" Public codes, from tax law to welfare policy, are rewritten and interpreted with the promotion of stable families as the goal. Education policy is shaped to give families choice and input and control and to actually teach ethics and values and marriage and parenting skills to supplement what kids learn at home. Marriage and adoption laws are rewritten to prioritize staying together and growing together. Politicians campaign on family issues and propose family-strengthening ideas at the heart of their campaigns.

We see glimpses of these directions in all three sectors, yet their full fruition still looks like some sort of unobtainable utopia. It can come about only through a consistent, wide overlay of family consciousness and a clear awareness of family consequences by larger institutions. This will not come about easily. We've been moving away from it for decades. And no specific list of recommendations would cover the full breadth of the problem. Nevertheless, the suggestions in the next section, even partially adopted and implemented, could make a difference to families and make it easier for us all to succeed in our new-millennium parenting.

"Thorn" Recommendations to Each Section of Larger Institutions

Every day, large private, public, and nonprofit institutions make countless thousands of decisions, policies, and choices of direction and orientation that affect families. If every manager, every policymaker, every decision-making officer of every large corporation could be implanted with a tiny microchip that did nothing but maintain awareness of family importance and consistently pose the question, "How will this impact families?," that would, in fact, turn the hearts of policymakers in the direction of family needs. The world we live in would rapidly begin to become a different and better place.

Since the implanted-chip approach isn't possible, we'll try the "thorn" approach. Each "directional recommendation" that follows is intended to be a little attention-getting thorn in the side of decision makers in any larger institution—to get their attention and prod them to consider their products, their pitches, their procedures, their priorities, and their patterns in light of the net effect they are having on families. This may look a lot like a wish list—a set of things most parents *wish* the broader society would do to help (or to stop hurting) families. Most of them aren't likely to happen anytime soon. But while we're fixing our own families, we can wish, we can wait, and in some cases we can even demand.

1. Family-Supportive Suggestions for Work and Professional Institutions

Families are being squeezed harder than ever before by corporate America. The corporate preoccupation with profit and stock price is driving short-term policies that will hurt everyone in the long run.

What should corporations do for families? In essence, they should wake up to the fact that screwing their employees is a very bad long-term policy—bad for everyone, including stockholders and top managers. The companies that emerge on top in the new millennium will be those that can attract and hold a loyal work force. And as the number of available workers declines, companies with reputations for greedy top management, low worker wages, long hours, and poor family benefits and flex options will be the big losers. Those who are getting away with it now will not get away with it for long.

At the very least, any midsize to large corporation should seek to offer its employees:

a. A fair wage and other compensation commensurate with the company's overall profitability (a truly enlightened company will plan a reasonable limit on the ratio between its CEO and its lowest-paid worker).

b. Real, well-publicized, and accessible job flexibility options that can accommodate the needs of parents and kids—the whole gamut from flex time to job sharing, from telecommuting to child and elder care, and from real maternity and paternity leave to shorter work weeks, all should be considered and fine-tuned and incorporated. Companies need to turn these catch phrases into accessible realities.

c. Location-transfer policies that do not uproot families against their will.

d. Job security that can be interrupted or threatened only by extreme incompetency on the part of the employee or extreme profitability stress on the employer.

2. Family-Supportive Recommendations for Financial Institutions

Nothing destroys families like debt. By making high-interest credit card debt so easily available to everyone, and particularly to young parents and college-age kids, banks and other financial institutions are putting a huge financial strain on families even as they increase the default rates that result in higher costs and interest rates for everyone.

Instead of offering "pre-approved" credit cards to us all and competing with one another to see who can create the most debt and charge the highest interest rates, financial institutions should take more responsibility for assisting families in learning and practicing sound fiscal policies.

All any bank officer needs to do to be more family supportive is to treat and advise all customers as he would his own children. If his college freshman son received unsolicited, pre-approved credit cards in the mail at his dorm, the father would say, "Cut them up and throw them away or if you want to use one to establish credit, get one with a low limit, not more than $1,000, use it for one purchase a month, and pay the bill each month before there is any interest." If his married daughter and son-in-law asked about consumer debt or credit cards, he would say, "Use a check or debit card for now and avoid any debt except for education or to buy a house."

If that same banker and his counterparts everywhere would give the same advice to everyone, countless families would be saved and spared the devastation of heavy consumer debt.

The best goal that banks and other financial institutions could adopt—a goal aimed at benefiting their customers and thus benefiting themselves over the long term—would be like a coin with two sides: (1) avoid any policy or practice that endangers or hurts family solvency; (2) actively develop and implement programs to assist and help families stay financially sound.

In their best light, financial institutions and their services are enormously important and helpful to families. They allow the purchase of homes, they facilitate savings and retirement, and they give security and provide for retirement, but their services are constructive and helpful to those who are financially responsible and destructive for those who are not.

Banks ought to take a longer and closer look at the market segment that uses credit unwisely and offer everything from simple educational tools to highly promoted debit cards as an alternative to credit cards. They should encourage businesses like hotels or car rental companies to accept debit cards as readily as credit cards. Financial institutions ought to begin to judge themselves not by how high their average interest rate is but by how many stable family economies they can assist, knowing that those families will become lifetime customers with resource levels that produce bank revenue through long-term growth and investing rather than through gouging short-term consumer interest.

3. Family-Supportive Suggestions for Advertising/Merchandising Institutions

Advertising/merchandising institutions hurt families in two broad and basic ways: (1) through marketing strategies that induce greed, encourage instant gratification, and cause the kind of overextension that endangers families economically and turns parents' attention and priorities outward rather than inward; and (2) by creating ads and other images that glorify casual sex, violence, and materialism—the very things that damage and divide families most.

Trying to imagine our advertising/merchandising institutions reversing these two things is so difficult that the two following suggestions will be instantly labeled impossible if not laughable. Still, we feel compelled to make them—first because that is what this book is about and second because this group of institutions and any company within it would actually gain substantial long-term benefits by following them.

a. Advertisers/merchandisers should honor moderation and actually advocate and teach delayed gratification: Push the benefits and well-being of saving and waiting rather than the quick thrill of credit buying, and list the full honest price and promote the savings of paying cash rather than hyping the half truths and false promises of monthly payments. Over time, short-term losses would be overcome by the long-term benefits from loyal consumers who appreciate the honesty and the motives.

b. Advertisers/merchandisers should create messages and images that are centered around values and positive emotions like love, loyalty, and personal integrity. These ads and messages probably cost more and require brighter creative input, but over time they will help implant the same respect, loyalty, and love *from* the consumer that they portray *to* him.

These two dramatic shifts, impossible as they sound, could benefit most marketing institutions over the long haul—and they would help save the family.

4. Family-Supportive Suggestions for Entertainment and Media Institutions

Perhaps the two most self-serving, delusional public lies of the last couple of decades have been (a) the tobacco industry saying smoking is not addictive and (b) the movie, music, and television industries saying they don't *influence* public or individual morality and behavior, they only reflect it and report on it.

In fact, the media has enormous influence over how we perceive ourselves and our world and over how we live within it. Those who say otherwise are trying to defend the indefensible.

There is a basic question with a surprising answer that leads to some challenging recommendations:

THE QUESTION:

Why is so much of our programming—our movies, TV, music, and other media—so full of violence and sex? And why are really good portrayals of values, families, and positive role models so hard to find?

THE ANSWER:

It's not as simple as "sex sells" or "people are drawn to violence" or "producers give people what they want." The fact is that really good movies, about positive and powerful things, do sell—as do truly great music and value-oriented, even spiritually related television. Even upbeat, positive-slant news is well received if it is well reported and well produced. Yet all of these are scarce. Why? Simply because the baser the emotion, the easier and cheaper it is to portray. You don't need a great script or great actors to depict sex and violence. It takes much more subtlety and much more artistic talent to get audiences or listeners to feel faith or fidelity than to feel titillation or terror. Media institutions, in it for the profit and for their own preservation, churn out the easy formula—the stuff they can produce cheaply and that they know will sell.

a. *Recommendations to writers/producers/directors:* Have the courage to attempt the portrayal of the more positive (and more difficult) emotions and characteristics. Take the risk of making something about honor or truth or courage rather than the safe bet of more sex and violence. Show the real and honest consequences of things. Actually think about the effect and influence on the consumer. Meet the challenge that is inherent in all creation: "Think more about the ultimate quality, effect, and legacy of what you make and less about the short-term profit."

b. *Recommendations to actors, artists, celebrities, "role models," and their agents and publicists:* Seek involvement with the significant rather than the seamy. And take opportunities to showcase the good. There are so many celebrities with strong families and strong views about priorities—sides we never see, partly because of privacy and partly because it's thought not sensational enough to sell. But in fact, there is a hunger for human interest things that we can connect to and identify with. If people knew as much about the "good" as about the "bad," we might all be amazed (and reassured) that there is more of the former than the latter.

c. *Recommendations to news producers and directors:* If every news director or Internet producer had a child he really loved—say a ten-year-old—and if he knew that child would see and hear everything he created, we would probably reach far higher standards in what comes at us as news and information. Show the good and the hopeful as well as the bad and the hopeless. Don't sugarcoat anything, but don't drape it in black either.

d. *Recommendations to funders and benefactors and to resources that are not "players" now but could be:* Most of what ends up on the big or small screen, or on the CD, starts off as writing. And writers write what they think will sell. And often the only buyers are the producer types already discussed who subscribe to the sex-and-violence theory. Grants and prizes, both of recognition and of remuneration, can stimulate a lot of better writing. Foundations, corporations, endowed universities, churches—any entities with resources and with a desire to impact entertainment positively—could (and should) set up some form of writing prize for scripts or books or lyrics that portray positive, family, and character-strengthening emotions and story lines. Any philanthropic or alternative-minded organization looking to maximize its reach and impact would have a hard time finding a more powerful way to allocate its resources.

5. Family-Supportive Recommendations for Information and Communication Institutions

The much-heralded information age in which we live gives us access to virtually everything. Unfortunately, there seems to be *more* access to the sensational and the seamy than to the deeper values and virtues of life. There seems to be no end to the filth, violence, and antivalue attitudes that flow through our phone lines and on to our monitors or into our eyes and ears from the Internet or from a 900 phone number.

With these institutions, it's hard even to know who to direct our parents' appeal to. There is no CEO of the Internet. On the Internet—unlike media, merchandising, or financial institutions—there is no centralized, small number of people who make the decisions about the messages that will be sent out. Everyone can put something on the Internet, and it seems as though everyone does! We can throw out a general appeal about how vulnerable our children are and how dangerous these messages can be, but not many of those whose preoccupation is violence and raw, random sex are going to listen.

Thus we have a classic situation where government is needed to protect people from other people. The Internet should be regulated and restricted at least to the same degree that network television is.

The three standard arguments against such regulation are: (1) freedom of expression; (2) people choose to pay for and receive the Internet, so they should be able to get what they want; (3) you can't regulate something that has so many diverse suppliers. The three arguments are weak. Freedom of expression always stops when it endangers others, as in the often-quoted example of yelling "Fire!" in a crowded theater. Lots of things we pay for, from magazines to movies to the mail, are regulated if children could have easy access to them. And despite how many providers or suppliers there are of various types of filth, the beauty of the information age is that we know exactly where to find those providers. If fines and criminal penalties were stiff enough, most of the worst material could be eliminated over a fairly short time frame.

6. Family-Supportive Suggestions for Political/Governmental Institutions

Government on all levels needs to reprioritize and to reorient itself to the service, protection, maintenance, and motivation of society's basic building block: the family. As always, there are two sides to this coin:

- Reviewing and reversing or eliminating policies that harm, undermine, or weaken parents and families.
- Creating policies, incentives, and options that protect, encourage, and strengthen families.

Some specifics for each:

a.   *Reversing Family-Unfriendly Policy*

    1.   Eliminate the "marriage tax" so two married people never pay more tax than those same two people as single individuals.

    2.   Get rid of no-fault divorce and other divorce laws that favor the convenience of the spouse rather than the welfare of the child.

    3.   Roll back any law that limits parental input and responsibility regarding educational choices for their children.

b.   *Creating Family-Friendly Policy*

Short term:

1.   Return child deductions on income tax to their 1950s levels (over $4,000 per child in today's dollars).

2.   Create and improve school/college IRAs and other deductions that allow families to pay for their children's education with pre-tax dollars.

3.   Regulate the Internet by allowing parents to easily and effectively screen *all* violence and pornography.

Having gone that far, let us go even farther out onto the limb of improbability and suggest two dramatic longer-term public policy changes that could alter the very fabric of how government impacts families (and vice versa):

1.   Give parents one additional vote (in local and national elections) for each of their under-eighteen children. This kind of parental power at the ballot box would cause politicians to pander to families like never before and would no doubt unleash a stunning list of creative, family-friendly ideas and proposals.

2.   Eliminate all federal and state income taxes, substituting value-added sales taxes on everything but food. This would reward sav-

ing and work, strengthening society and rewarding families for the very prudence and industry that could strengthen the overall economy. It would also eliminate the enormous IRS and state income tax bureaucracies and refocus a huge section of the legal establishment.

7. *Family-Supportive Suggestions for Educational Institutions*

We live in a society that requires licensing or training or registration for almost every conceivable activity. We even need a license to fish. Yet anyone—with no license, no training, and all too often no sense of responsibility—can assume the most critical and important role that exists in society: that of a parent. Children receive no formal training on how to become responsible parents. And most parents receive no instruction or training on how to improve. Our schools—probably the only institution close enough and influential enough to collectively wake kids up to the responsibility and importance of parenting or to offer widely available instruction to parents—have done very little to help young people appreciate and be prepared for the role of parents. In fact, they do much that is negative and counterproductive to sexual responsibility and commitment. And schools have not recognized their opportunity and responsibility to help parents know more about parenting.

The most sweeping and positive thing all public and private elementary and secondary teachers could do is to *see* themselves as the closest, most accessible, and most important backups, safety nets, and teammates to parents (not as substitutes, but as supports). When schools and teachers think of their role and their job as one of *helping* parents raise responsible and educated children, schools become better, parents become better, and most important, *children* become both better and happier. Here's what schools should strive harder to do for parents and for kids:

A. FOR PARENTS:

1. Offer evening or weekend classes on parenting and specifically on how to help a child succeed academically.

2. Put on more family functions where kids come to school with parents—from the traditional sports, plays, and social events to creative academic and community events, and from read-a-thons and back-to-school nights to service projects. Offer special family prices to every school function that has an admittance charge.

3. Improve parent-teacher conferences and schedule options where parents can come in with their child to work out a teamwork approach to learning.

B. FOR CHILDREN:

1. Have a mandatory course on ethics and values in the seventh grade. Plenty of good curriculums and programs exist. Rotate the teaching (a math teacher teaches it one semester, a history teacher the next), thus reaching out and transplanting values into the texture and content of other classes.

2. Have a required class on parenting and family responsibility for all high school juniors. Teach marriage and parenting skills, but also teach family and relationship priorities.

3. Incorporate personal and family responsibility into all sex education classes. Reorient the curriculums so there are classes about what families are and what they should be, and about the importance of commitment and responsibility. Within this framework, sex education, human intimacy, and reproductive facts take on a whole new and more positive slant. Involve the parents who are willing to become involved—and at least inform the rest.

8. *Family-Supportive Suggestions for Courts and Legal Institutions*

We're dealing with two related but separate institutions here: first, the court system of America and its judicial process, which has increasingly interpreted laws in a way that overemphasizes individual autonomy at the expense of what is best for families and parents. Second, the institution of private law firms and attorneys, which has made divorce, separation, and litigation too prominent on the family landscape.

A. JUDGES AND THEIR COURTS NEED TO:

1. Re-enshrine the family and reflect (in their opinions) interpretations of laws that respect the responsibility and stewardship of parents.

2. Favor the welfare and well-being of children rather than the convenience of parents in divorce or other domestic disputes.

3. Strive for better balance between protecting the rights of individuals and children and preserving the unity, autonomy, and priority of families.

B. WITH REGARD TO PRIVATE LEGAL PRACTICE, WE NEED TO:

1. Close down a few law schools—quit producing so many litigators. As an alternate to fewer law schools, just discontinue some of the divorce law and litigation courses and substitute more instruction on arbitration mediation and alternative conflict resolution.

2. Do all we can to persuade the legal establishment that remains that their job is to save families, not pull them apart. Focus more on win-win arbitration and less on win-lose (or lose-lose) litigation, and always view divorce and family breakup as a last resort.

9. *Family-Supportive Suggestions for Recreation and Social/Cultural Institutions*

Recreation and social life not only used to revolve around the family, it used to occur primarily within the immediate and extended family. Today, enormous recreational and social/cultural institutions consume and suck away what used to be family time and fracture the family through different interests and options that take family members in different directions. Play, diversion, and social and cultural activities—the very things that should bring families together and add richness and diversity to family life—have begun to do the opposite.

Once again, a new mindset by those who manage and run the institutionalized recreation and cultural establishments could make a positive and powerful difference to families. Directions that ought to receive consideration:

a. Stop scheduling everything on Sunday. Sundays are still the best chance for most families to be at home (or at church) together. With everything from soccer games to kids' recitals spilling into Sunday, private family time is even more scarce.

We lived in England for four years in the seventies and eighties. In that era, everything was closed on Sundays. No stores were open except the occasional emergency pharmacy, and no sporting or musical events occurred. Even the British Open golf tournament and Wimbledon had their finals on Saturday and had no play on Sunday. This had a remarkable effect on our family. Our only option was to do family things together. We went on long walks, played family games, went to church together. Sundays became a true and refreshing change of pace—something we have never been able to duplicate here at home in the United States.

b. Give "real deals" to families who come together. If more spectator events—from high school sports to movies—offered family passes or major discounts for family groups, it would increase ticket sales even as it brought more families together.

   c. Request and encourage volunteering, especially family volunteering. There is nothing quite like volunteering as a family. Working together in a good cause—whether it's serving food at a homeless shelter or cleaning up a park or roadway—really brings parents and children together. Voluntary agencies and community service organizations should aim more of their outreach and recruiting at families and create projects where parents and children can volunteer together.

One of our daughters has recently been working for Family Matters, the family-volunteering arm of the Points of Light Foundation in Washington, D.C. Their effort is to reach out and encourage families to sign up for volunteer projects together so they can combine family time and parent-child communication opportunities with the community service they render.

   Parents who have become involved indicate that in addition to the satisfaction of service and the quality family time, they have had amazing opportunities to teach values like empathy, love, and self-reliance to their children.

   d. Create recreational options that revolve around family and the parent-child relationship. Instead of camps, sports leagues, church outings, and music retreats that take kids away from parents, organizers should try to come up with occasional alternatives that let parent and child attend and participate together.

10. Family-Supportive Recommendations for Religious Institutions (and Psychological, Self-Help, and Counseling Sectors)

Historically, it is religion that people have looked to for help with their families as well as their spiritual well-being and their outlooks and philosophies of life. During the last several decades self-help, psychiatry, and other secular counseling have become important factors as well.

   The question is, are religious and counseling institutions doing their job? Are they working? Are they playing as strong and prominent a role a they should in saving, safeguarding, and stabilizing families? Or are some of the elements of these institutions working against families by stressing and glamorizing individual freedom and autonomy at the expense of family connections, responsibilities, interdependencies, and commitments?

We hear far too little of churches speaking out strongly against antifamily messages, models, and media. We see divorce becoming easier and more acceptable in faith communities. We see all sorts of affairs, amorality, and alternative lifestyles being tolerated if not sanctioned by religions. It seems that many of our religious institutions have become so anxious to attract and recruit parishioners and so overcommitted to tolerance that they no longer try very hard to make it clear what is right and what is wrong—both in the eyes of God and in terms of what is good and bad for the family. We are forgetting the wisdom and insight expressed by G. K. Chesterton, who said, "Tolerance is the favorite virtue of those who don't believe in anything."

Counseling and self-help entities, on the other hand, are more and more involved and prominent in trying to fix what ails us. Yet so often what they offer is a "quick fix" that essentially sets us up for a fall.

Essentially, our churches, synagogues, mosques, and other religious institutions have to step up and be stronger and bolder in their advocacy of the family and in training, assisting, and helping parents. At the very least, churches should:

a. Formally and emphatically make recommitments to the sanctity and pivotal importance of the family, reminding all that family priority and mutual fidelity lie at the heart of God's teaching.

b. Establish more extensive programs for parenting education, for teaching family communication, and for providing spiritually based marriage and family counseling.

c. Speak out more strongly and vigorously against early casual, recreational sex (scripturally, fornication) and marital infidelity (scripturally, adultery). Talk more openly about the devastation sexual irresponsibility brings to families.

By the same token, secular counselors, authors, and analysts need to understand that individual "solutions" without some connection or acknowledgment of family are doomed to failure over the long term.

Too much is being written and spoken about avoiding co-dependency, developing self-confidence, and building wealth, and too little is being written and spoken about building positive family interdependency, developing empathy and faith, and building strong families. Writers, therapists, and "gurus" of all kinds should:

a. Ponder the long-term and the ultimate importance of family relationships to be sure their recommended "quick fixes" don't work at odds with what really matters.

b. Examine their own motives to be certain what they are preaching and recommending stems from their genuine belief in what is best for people over their whole lives and not from their own desire for short-term profit and popularity.

Turning the Hearts/Revaluing Families

How many of these and other similar family-supportive suggestions are ever implemented (or even taken seriously) by policymakers of larger institutions really depends on where the *hearts* of these individuals are. When our hearts are turned to family, when we feel those warm longings, those tender feelings that come from the best part of us—feelings of unconditional love and undying commitment to our children and our spouses—that is when we begin to make a difference in our own homes and in our broader roles in the larger society. And when we think clearly, whether as a parent or as a CEO, we realize that one consideration we should have in everything we do is the goal to revalue families.

This book won't convince a film producer to make a more moral, more uplifting movie—but his love for his own child might. A printed suggestion won't persuade the president of a bank to cut back on easy credit—but her love for her own family might.

And so it goes. Everything starts with the heart. As parents' hearts turn to children, as children's hearts turn to parents, families change. And as families change, the world changes, the curse lifts, and life has meaning.

Essential Element Twelve: Find a Support Group

Parents who finish this book with a genuine desire to protect and improve their families—parents whose hearts turn—are going to need one additional thing beyond their own rededication. They are going to need some kind of support group to encourage and sustain and support their rekindled parenting and family efforts.

The adage "It takes a village to raise a child," while used too often and too politically, nonetheless is absolutely true in the context that parents need other adults—individually and in groups—as allies and as support mechanisms in their effort to raise happy and responsible children. For one thing, we all need moral and emotional support and encouragement (and commiseration). Parenting can be a lonely process where we are prone to think that nobody has problems or challenges like ours. Sometimes just knowing other parents who *do* gives us the courage to keep trying. And second, we just plain need help in the form of other caring adults who will genuinely try to help teach our kids the same things we are teaching them. As parents, we know that our children will often accept something from another adult more quickly and more easily than they will accept it from us. It's the whole concept of "other mentors" and "other examples" that gives weight and credibility to what we try to teach.

Frankly, the best parental support group is usually a neighborhood church, synagogue, or mosque. Through services, classes, youth activities, and various other forms of guidance and mentoring, children receive solid secondary support. And parents get instruction, insight, and encouragement, along with the ability and opportunity to share ideas and concerns with other parents. This certainly is not the only reason for finding a plan of worship in which you can be comfortable and active, but it is one very good reason.

A neighborhood church that helps teach children (as well as ourselves) correct principles, basic values, and faith can be the ideal "second ring" that surrounds and supports the family and that supplements parents in many of the eleven essential elements.

A scout troop, a boys and girls club, a community center, or an active PTA or parents auxiliary group of some kind can also serve the support group function.

An additional form of support and motivation can come from join-ing some kind of parenting co-op or organization set up with the exclu-sive purpose of supporting and assisting parents. Some such groups exist in communities, some on the Internet. We have our own, called SJS HOMEBASE or valuesparenting.com, which we organized more than twenty years ago and which now has a membership of over 100,000 par-ents. It supplies: 1. a monthly family and parenting newsletter; 2. materi-als for neighborhood "Joy Schools," where parents alternate as the volunteer preschool teacher of a curriculum of twelve social and emo-tional "joys" (i.e. the Joy of Sharing and Service, the Joy of Imagination and Creativity, etc.); and 3. a set of twelve monthly "values units," involv-ing a child's and parent's tape on each of twelve basic values; and 4. an Internet site where parents receive everything from weekly parenting tips to the opportunity to participate in parent-to-parent chat rooms. The most important benefit of SJS HOMEBASE groups is that they bring par-ents together where they can share ideas and concerns as well as the responsibility of helping out with each other's children. More and more, SJS HOMEBASE will also be involved with attempts to push for imple-mentation of some of this book's "Family Supportive Suggestions" in larger institutions.

Call (801) 581-0112 for a free membership information packet or get the same information online at www.valuesparenting.com.

Notes

1. How we live poll, *The New York Times Magazine*, May 7, 2000 (conducted by Blum and Weprin Associates, Inc.), p. 66.

2. Yankelovich "Priceless Poll," done for MasterCard, Inc. in 1999.

3. How we live poll, p. 90.

4. Newsweek poll, *Newsweek*, May 8, 2000, p. 56.

5. How we live poll, p. 56.

6. Ibid., p. 56.

7. Ibid., p. 56.

8. Ibid., p. 66.

9. *The Wall Street Journal*, November 14, 1997, p. 86.

10. *The New York Times*, April 14, 1997, p. 6.

11. Romesh Ratnesar, "The Iceman Cometh," *Mother Jones*, November/December 1995, p. 2.

12. David M. Gordon, *Fat and Mean: The Corporate Squeeze of Working Americans and the Myth of Managerial "Downsizing"* (New York: Free Press, 1996), pp. 34, 42.

13. *New York Times*, July 23, 1997, p. 23.

14. Lester G. Thurow, *The Future of Capitalism* (New York: Morrow, 1996) p. 24.

15. *USA Today*, April 29, 1999, p. D-1.

16. *New York Times*, June 18, 1996, p. D-1.

17. Thurow, *The Future of Capitalism*, p. 27.

18. John Stinson, Economist, Bureau of Labor Statistics, reported by Sylvia Ann Hewlett and Cornel West in *The War Against Parents* (New York: Houghton Mifflin, 1998) p. 71.

19. Juliet B. Schorr, *The Overworked American* (New York: Basic Books, 1992), p. 29.

20. Gordon, *Fat and Mean: The Corporate Squeeze of Working Americans and the Myth of Managerial "Downsizing,"* p. 204.

21. How we live poll, p. 58.

22. *USA Today*, "Snapshots," May 7, 2000.

23. Richard and Linda Eyre, *Three Steps to a Strong Family* (New York: Simon & Schuster, 1994.)

24. George Gallup, Jr., and D. Michael Lindsay, *Surveying the Religious Landscape* (Harrisburg, Penn.: Morehouse Publishing, 1999), pp. 24, 25.

Richard and Linda Eyre have co-authored eight books (including the *New York Times* number-one bestseller *Teaching Your Children Values*) and co-parented nine children (who they think of as their greatest credential as well as their greatest joy). The Eyres live in Salt Lake City, Utah, and McLean, Virginia. They lecture throughout the world on the topics of family, balance, and the spirit.